THINKING ABOUT TEACHING AND LEARNING

THINKING ABOUT TEACHING AND LEARNING

Developing Habits of Learning with First Year College and University Students

Robert Leamnson

Stty/us

STERLING, VIRGINIA

Published by
STYLUS PUBLISHING, LLC.
22883 Quicksilver Drive
Sterling, Virginia 20166-2012

Library of Congress Cataloging-in-Publication Data
Leamnson, Robert N.
    Thinking about teaching and learning: developing
habits of learning with first year college and university
students / Robert Leamnson. — 1st ed.
        p.   cm.
    Includes bibliographical references (p.   ) and index.
    ISBN 1-57922-012-6 (alk. paper)
    ISBN 1-57922-013-4 (pbk.: alk. paper)
    1. Colleges teaching.   2. Learning.   3. College
student orientation.   4.   Effective teaching.   I. Title.
LB2331.L39   1999
378.1'2—dc21

                                         98–39114
                                           CIP

Hard cover ISBN: 1-57922-012-6
Paper back ISBN: 1-57922-013-4

Printed in USA on acid free paper.

Reprinted 2000, 2001, 2003, 2004

Design by POLLEN

CONTENTS

To Brian and Ann

The impetus to write a book on teaching came after I heard a colleague give her retirement address at a faculty convocation. She said that during her first twenty years of teaching she hadn't noticed significant year-to-year differences in the abilities of incoming first-year students. However, she had noted that in the last ten years there had been a notable decline. She summarized the difference as an inability to cope with the culture of the university. Subsequent research suggested that her observations (which mirrored my own) were not imaginary. Teaching first year students in college or university was becoming decidedly more difficult.

Comprehensive plans to address the problem of unprepared students are in the works, but are many years from being available. In the meantime, teaching must go on. Teachers must do what teachers do. I consider it the teacher's obligation to do the best possible with whatever we are given—we hardly have a choice.

The purpose of this book is not to eliminate the present difficulties, or to explain them away, but to turn the bright light of critical inquiry on them and exhort teachers of beginning college students to see the difficulties for what they are, and then to do what needs to be done. The audience for this book may not be familiar with the hypotheses and theories of contemporary education, but they are nevertheless looking for some answers to the problems they face teaching first-time college or university students.

There are a number of things that teachers can do to help students get into the higher education learning mode, but they are generally difficult. This is not a problem awaiting a solution—it is simply a tough job that desperately needs doing.

There are hypothetical answers to the problem of underprepared students entering college. Studies and reports on elementary and secondary education are plentiful, and they usually end with answers that are obviously correct but impossible to implement. If young people of all ages learned by means of reading and writing, for example, the problem of preparedness for college would be reduced to easily manageable proportions. But that is as useful as the observation that if we all behaved properly we would not need laws. The hypothetical part, the "if" part, simply isn't there.

I write to draw attention to what we know about students, teaching, and learning. I have draped my opinions and observations on a framework of basic assumptions that underlie my reasoning. These underpinnings will be briefly commented on here as they may not always be obvious in what follows.

Play the Hand You're Dealt

Trying to undo what's been done will not prove productive. We can restore, we can repair damage, but we can't undo history. There is nothing to be gained, therefore, by dwelling on our students' prior schooling. But neither can we be content with them as we find them. Seeing them as flawed vessels will only tempt us to pour in what we can and hope it doesn't all leak out. The more constructive view is that they are neither finished nor vessels, but works in progress, perhaps behind schedule and maybe in need of some retrofitting. As teachers we might think of ourselves as being in the business of restoration. The more a thing has been neglected, the greater the satisfaction in bringing it to a state of usefulness or beauty. First-year students might not be ready for us, but there they are, a hundred strong and at our feet, waiting for us to do something.

Teaching Improves if It Is Based on a Sound Philosophy

Anyone setting out to teach has a philosophy of teaching. Philosophy does not imply anything esoteric or grand. Philosophy means only those things we hold to be true about students, about the process of learning, and about what we should be doing to teach well. Nothing so complex and unpredictable as teaching should be done without thinking about it. And it is from thinking about it, and seeing what others have thought and said about it, as well as actually doing it, that a philosophy of teaching develops. I here make a suggestion that will be repeated several times in the following pages—knowledge of one's discipline is not in itself sufficient for presenting it in a way that will inspire students to learn. One of the intended outcomes of a philosophy of teaching is pedagogy—what it is we actually do when we teach. A further implication is that a philsophy can be mistaken, in that the beliefs it implies might not correspond with reality. It takes some effort to arrive at a sound philosophy of teaching.

Getting Ready to Learn is Part of Learning

A major difficulty in teaching first-year students is getting them up to speed. Were college learning no different from students' previous educational experience there would be no complaining from college instructors, no orientation programs, and certainly no need for books such as this. Most of what will follow is based on the perception that most first-year students do not know how to listen well, to make notes on what they hear, to read with comprehension, or to write referentially about the real world. Nonetheless, an equally important premise is that they are completely capable of learning to do all of these things. How we go about teaching these students will be determined in large part by whether we see them as being ruined past repair, or as works in progress—unfinished and by varying degrees behind schedule. If the latter, you'll then believe that, though taxing, the work will be possible.

Strategy is Knowing Where to Strike

One way to address the deficiencies we find in first-year students might be called the identify, isolate, and remediate approach. Most of us would like our students to come to us fresh out of an academic boot camp as well-oiled learning machines. Remedial courses in writing, mathematics, and critical thinking would appear to fit the bill. But remedial courses that address perceived deficiencies have been around long enough to allow research on their efficacy. The results are not particularly encouraging. These courses purport to instill "transferable skills," but it's the transferable part that eludes demonstration. It's becoming more and more obvious that desirable skills need to be learned within the context of some real academic content.

More likely to succeed than sending students to remedial courses, is to find a "nodal problem" (described in chapter 6)—some deficiency that blocks all the other skills we would hope to find in first-year students. My candidate for a nodal problem is language use. The typical beginning college student is marginally equipped to deal with the language of any discipline at the college level, whether in verbal discourse, reading, or writing. The language obstacle is central to all the arguments I present in this book.

A Student is a Package Deal

Most of us learn, sometimes slowly, sometimes painfully, that the people we interact with—spouses, lovers, offspring, colleagues, supervisors—are unique individuals with their own of characteristics, predilections, and personality traits. So it is that a student might be brilliant and irresponsible or illiterate and charming. The student is a whole person.

We do our best work when we provide whatever help is most needed. This implies some degree of personal knowlede of the individuals we teach, and an appreciation of young people in general. While the average age of students entering college is generally increasing, most first-year students are still quite young adults—almost adults. They are our lumpy raw material. To be effective as teachers we must deal with first-year students in all aspects of their person, their strengths, their faults and their shortcomings. We might have to do more for students now than we would have in the past, but this is the hand that we have been dealt.

It's safe to assume that our students are also beginning to appreciate the satisfaction that comes from having mature friends and they may see their teachers as possible candidates. Teaching is more satisfying if we, in turn, like our students. And if we do like them, the majority will respond in kind.

Nothing New Under the Sun

I don't believe that there is much about teaching that can be called new. Certainly the appearance of computers, electronic classrooms, distance learning and the like are all new technologies and many teachers will have to learn some new tricks to take advantage of the technology. But I consider technologies and techniques in general to be more peripheral than central to the business of teaching. It is the "core of education," to use Elmore's (1996) phrase, that remains unchanged. This core is what it always has been, a personal interaction between teacher and student, no matter the technology. When students and their learning problems become central, technologies, methods, and techniques, both new and old, will be used with reason.

New teaching innovations are largely sound practices dusted off and updated. For example, cooperative learning has been practiced with great benefit for many years, but it is now getting wide exposure and more formal organization. Active learning has always been, for most teachers, the only kind there was, but now it is becoming more formalized and consciously practiced.

All of the ideas presented in these pages can be traced to sources going back as much as a hundred years or more. The notion of considering teaching and learning as difficulties rather than unsolved problems comes from Jacques Barzun (1991). The concept of a nodal problem is that of Ortega y Gasset (1987), and language as a nodal problem comes from Neil Postman (1969). Seeing students as nice people coming to us with their problems was an idea thoroughly treated many years ago by Gilbert Highet (1966). The mistake of expecting students to be prepared was previously noted by Jerome Bruner (1968).

This book aspires to present, to an audience not normally inclined to read books on pedagogy, some connections between sound traditional learning processes and ways of teaching both old or new. The focus is on students just entering college or university, the group most in need of attention and so the greatest challenge,.

In chapter 1 I present reasons for thinking about teaching and ways to develop a sustaining but responsive philosophy. This is followed by a detailed exposition of what I consider learning to be (chapter 2), and the part language plays in learning (chapter 3). To better appreciate the challenge college presents to new students (and they to us), I've included a somewhat somber section (chapter 4) on the culture students come from and their habits of mind, particularly with respect to language, goals, responsibility, and schooling in general. Chapters 5, 6, and 7 describe a collection of practices that incorporate my convictions about teaching, learning, and language. Chapter 8 presents some thoughts on how our efforts to teach well fit into the overall scheme of things in today's college or university, particularly with regard to evaluations, assessments, and career goals.

ACKNOWLEDGMENTS

I welcome the opportunity to thank Jack Donner and Beth Kessler of Pollen Design for careful editing and design, and Mark Wasserman and Maryellen Weimer for reviewing early drafts, and for helpful suggestions. Brian Wilkie, deftly handling his longstanding dual role as friend and critic, read nearly every page of the manuscript and spared me many an embarrassment, for which I am very grateful. It has been a joy to work with John von Knorring of Stylus Publishing. With a light hand on the reins he has been an unfailing source of good advice and encouragement throughout the many months this book was in preparation.

Robert Leamnson
Dartmouth, Massachusetts
December, 1998

I

THINKING ABOUT
THINKING ABOUT TEACHING

It is a serious thing to interfere with
another man's life.
                    —*Gilbert Highet*

On my office desk I keep a stash of jelly beans in a glass jar. The jar is direct-ly behind me and out of my sight when I'm using the computer. For weeks, one senior student, whom I will call Tim, tried repeatedly to slip into the room, remove the jar lid, extract a jelly bean or two, replace the lid, and make his escape undetected while I worked at the computer. Time and again I would hear a footstep, or the clink of glass, or the soft rustle of purloined jelly beans. Without looking I would call out, "Tim, get out of those jelly beans!" Tim would mutter, "Damn!" and, mouth stuffed with the ill-gotten goods, make an embarrassed retreat. Eye witnesses tell me that he eventually succeeded, to the great delight of his friends.

The Tims of the world have sustained my interest in teaching at both the secondary and college level for nearly forty years. They approach learning with the same curiosity, persistence, intensity and playfulness that Tim brought to the challenge of pilfering jelly beans. I fully understand Gilbert Highet's (1966) observation, "It's easy to like the young because they are young. They have no faults, except the very ones which they are asking you to eradicate: ignorance, shallowness, and inexperience." Overstated perhaps, but his point is well taken.

For all the pleasure they have afforded me, the Tims are, unfortunately, a minority. Curious and hard-working students are also forgotten when criticisms are leveled at college, and by extension, college teaching. When the critics' subject is college graduates, an old adage is reversed. The successes are orphans and the failures have a thousand fathers.

Most college teachers are fond of people like Tim, and teaching with such students is a joy. But it is also true that these same students make teaching relatively easy. It's the others who need attention.

New College Students

Teaching at any level implies pedagogy, even if it is unplanned or unconscious, because pedagogy is just a word for the summation of our teaching behaviors. Teaching might demand more preparation as the content matter becomes more difficult, but the teaching itself becomes difficult when, to achieve its ends, it demands pedagogy that is not simply spontaneous, but developed with great care to cope with specific circumstances. Highly motivated students in their last year of college work might still appreciate variety and other results of a well-planned pedagogy, but they do not, by and large, rely on it to learn. They need only be told what's important. They have, in short, learned how to learn, and are able to cope with the simplest of pedagogies—a knowledgeable teacher telling them what they need to know.

How such students got to be that way is certainly some mix of nature and nurture. But anyone who has had the opportunity to teach the same students at both the beginning and the end of their college career will have noticed changes that are significant and sometimes dramatic. Students' genetic endowments not having changed, we can safely conclude that their college experiences—the teachers they had and the courses they took—have had considerable impact.

It is also true, however, that such admirable students are not representative of their entering cohort. On average only about half the matriculating first-year college students ever graduate. The sizable attrition rate suggests that typical first-year college students—those coming directly from secondary education—are not well prepared for college learning.

First-year students present the greatest challenge to college and university teachers. So while these pages contain a number of general observations and reflections on teaching and learning, emphasis is on the special problems of teaching first-year students. The title of this book suggests its central message—that all college instructors, particularly those who teach first-year students, would do well to consider and reflect, not only on what they teach, but how they teach, and what effects their pedagogy has on their students.

The word "teaching" would seem to be almost self explanatory, but in fact it can mean quite different things to different people. I will give some extended definitions of teaching, learning, and education in chapter 5, but, to ensure that my intent is clear, I will make explicit here my own use of the word teaching. In these pages *teaching* means *any activity that has the conscious intention of, and potential for, facilitating learning in another*. An obvious fallout of this expansive definition is that no distinction is yet being made as to the quality or effectiveness of the teaching.

Pedagogy will refer not to intent or potential, but to the specific activities and behaviors of teachers as they teach or prepare to teach. Every teacher, then, has pedagogical methods whether or not they call them by that name, or are even consciously aware of them.

Building a Philosophy of Teaching

Every teacher, even the beginner, has a philosophy of teaching. We all enter the classroom, even the first time, with certain beliefs about how teaching should be done. These beliefs might or might not be well-considered and articulated, but even the first-time teacher, trying to recall what his or her teachers did, is exhibiting some belief as to how teaching is done. In the case of experienced teachers, where a philosophy has had more time to develop, the philosophy might be passive—practices and methods built over time and from experience but without much planning.

At first glance a philosophy developed entirely out of experience might seem a good thing. But a philosophy so derived is primarily reactive, meaning that it evolved entirely from student responses to teaching behaviors. Philosophy and pedagogy arrived at in this way are sometimes defended as being responsive to students' needs. In the field of contemporary education, responding to students' needs is a good thing. But less clearly articulated is who is best equipped to determine what those needs are. That students are the best arbiters of their *academic* needs is highly questionable. Most students have goals, but these are usually long-term and nebulous, and are better described as wishes for the future. Students' academic goals are pretty much limited to getting into the school and major of their choice, getting a degree, and maintaining a certain grade point average. You are not likely to encounter a first-year student who expresses a need to learn a foreign language, some math, psychology, something about human institutions, or chemistry. In general, first-year students have little knowledge of what they need to learn in order to achieve their long-term goals. Their interests tend more toward credentialing than learning. Deciding what students need to learn in order to achieve their long term goals is our job.

This aspect of a teacher's philosophy (determining what needs to be learned) is a fairly obvious one. Less obvious and frequently less considered is the new students' need to become acclimated to college work and the new and (usually) more demanding expectations they face. John Gardner and his associates at the University of South Carolina, through their "Freshman Year Experience" programs, have been laboring for years to draw attention to the great difficulty many first-year students have in adjusting. Their efforts have sensitized many institutions to the transition problem. Awareness of a problem is not tantamount to solving it, however. Many colleges see this transition as a matter of orientation, a softer word, without the ring of permanence associated with transition. Often orientation consists of a few days of intense activities before classes begin, and a nonacademic (sometimes optional) orientation course in the first semester. Meritorious and congenial as these programs are, they do, I think, expect too much of themselves. For most students college demands major adjustments in learning styles, study habits, use of free time, and interacting as adults with their teachers. These changes all involve substantial modification of long-standing habits. They will come about, if at all, over a considerable time span, and with persistent vigilance on the part of all concerned.

Teaching first-year students is so different from teaching the more experienced, that we need to develop an explicit philosophy or set of beliefs for teaching the first-year student. Ideally, all teachers of college freshmen would consider themselves a major component in the year-long and demanding process of acculturating first-year students to a new way of life. The need is so acute that I have chosen to address it almost exclusively in the following chapters.

The philosophy I'm suggesting addresses the specific needs of first-year students, but that does not imply that there is a one-size-fits-all philosophy that can be formulated once and for all and applied as needed. As surely as students differ one from another so do teachers, disciplines, and institutions. A philosophy of teaching for first-year students is influenced by all of these elements. However, there are certain difficulties that students have in their first-year that are sufficiently common that any freshman teacher developing or reconsidering a philosophy of teaching can take them into account. These include pre-college culture, study habits, and a refractory mind-set about schooling in general (all of these will be addressed in later chapters).

The real goal of teaching is that someone learn. Having a goal, however, is not the same as having a philosophy. Our beliefs, or hunches, as to what learning is, how it's accomplished, who or what motivates it, and how it is demonstrated or assessed are all components of our philosophy of teaching. But, where do these beliefs come from? Are they well-considered? Have they been tested? Experienced teachers can answer that their beliefs have been tested in the classroom. But I draw on my own considerable classroom experience to suggest that experience alone is not an adequate source for developing a good teaching philosophy. We stand on the shoulders of giants who have much to offer us.

A rational and considered philosophy of teaching serves as a beacon during stormy periods. And there will be such periods, particularly with first-year students. Because so many of them do not really know what's in their best interests, your efforts can put you at cross purposes with their desires. It is for that reason that a useful philosophy of teaching cannot be just reactive. A philosophy that develops in a reactive way and completely out of experience runs the risk of producing a pedagogy that merely accommodates students' felt needs.

Learning Defined

Which brings us face to face with a major conflict that can develop between energetic and well-intentioned teachers and their first-year students. To consider this idea, it will be necessary to introduce here the definition of learning that I will use consistently in these pages. As was the case with *teaching*, the definition of learning will simply be stated here: a more thorough explication will appear in chapter 5. *Learning* is defined as *stabilizing, through repeated use, certain appropriate and desirable synapses in the brain*. This definition implies that learning is not exactly easy. Building new brain connections requires effort as surely as does building muscles. Students do not understand learning in these terms. And because the results cannot be seen in a mirror, the value of permanent brain change is lost on many. Like anyone else, they will avoid strenuous effort if there appears to be no point to it.

The danger, then, of a completely reactive philosophy of teaching is that it can produce a pedagogy that maximizes a student's comfort level—a situation that is not compatible with learning. My caution against a purely reactive philosophy of teaching might seem at odds with Stephen Brookfield's (1990) suggestion that our teaching rationale should be "responsive." But there is no real disagreement here. No philosophy worked out before the fact, no matter how keenly reasoned, could possibly anticipate the messiness of trying to get new college students to learn. By "responsive" Brookfield means that even the most carefully designed philosophy will need to be tweaked when experience demonstrates that some element of pedagogy, derived from that philosophy, is simply not producing the expected learning. I fully agree. I use "reactive" in the pejorative sense of being accommodating—adjusting one's beliefs to coincide with students' desires. To be responsive in Brookfield's sense, a teacher would first have to take a hard look at students' desires to see if these are really in their best interests. What we are both saying is that adjustments to our beliefs and practices should be made only on the basis of their effectiveness in promoting learning.

What I have been calling a philosophy of teaching is close to what others have called a "personal vision" (Brookfield) or a "critical rationale" (Smyth 1986). Brookfield's statement of the need is worth quoting. "A critical rationale is a set of values, beliefs, and convictions about the essential forms and fundamental purposes of teaching."

That both experienced and inexperienced teachers need to think about what they want to accomplish by teaching, who it is that needs to learn, how learning comes about, and what part teaching plays in learning, is not, then, an original idea. Indeed, those books and monographs on teaching that I find most inspiring and influential all build their arguments more around philosophy than theory. In general the authors of these works assume that teachers set out consciously to change the lives of their students. That being the case, it is crucially important that we have clear ideas on how we would like our students to change and what we can do to best help them. And as Highet (1966) reminds us, changing peoples' lives is serious business.

If our philosophy includes knowledge of and beliefs about our students, it follows that it will be somewhat different for different groups. Certainly what we believe to be true for seniors who are self-motivated and fully acculturated to college learning will be different from what we believe to be true of first-year students. It follows that we may have to teach differently for first year students than for the more experienced.

Philosophy Influences Pedagogy

A set of beliefs is hardly worthy of the name if those beliefs do not inform behavior. It's unlikely that anyone would teach without thinking about it— on automatic pilot so to speak. (Lee Shulman refers to this as "drive by pedagogy.") I believe that people who teach college want to be as effective as possible. For something as complex and unpredictable as teaching, we would do well to think about teaching, read about teaching, and talk about teaching reflectively, honestly, and seriously. So I will end this introduction with my own personal minimal list of elements that should go into a philosophy of teaching. Readers are encouraged to consider it and make amendments appropriate to the situations they find themselves in.

1. *Develop a clear and explicit concept of what learning is.*

    Learning cannot be discussed and thought about as a nebulous or mystical process that we know nothing about.

2. *Language is at the heart of the matter.*

    Critical thinking, good citizenship, good jobs and all the other goals of education depend entirely on the accurate transmission of ideas from one to another, and that can only be done with language.

3. *Beware the "preposterism."*

    This is Jacques Barzun's term for trying to go directly to the goal without traversing the means (1991).

4. *Know the clientele.*

    Students must be known as they come to us and not as we would like them to be. Knowing includes their culture, their level of preparedness, and their real intellectual and emotional needs.

5. *Believe that what you do makes a difference.*

    What we do is different from what we know. How we present our discipline to students is as important as what we present.

6. *If it sounds too good to be true it probably is.*

    There are certainly quick and easy ways to get students active and attentive, but the learning part is never quick and easy.

7. *Helping implies loving.*

    We work hard and go that extra mile for those we love. We will go about our teaching more seriously and energetically if we love our students.

What follows grows out of these philosophical ideas, but delves into pedagogy as well, because I am convinced, and I would ask the reader to consider the possibility, that one way is not as good as another when the activity is teaching, and no one way works in every case. Theories about teaching and learning are plentiful. Not all of them have had the benefit of rigorous testing. Mischief can be done by embracing untested educational hypotheses. Latching on to some innovative technique as the answer to the riddle is not recommended. Brookfield's observation in this regard is, again, to the point and well taken. "Sometimes what most hinders students' learning is a teacher's determination to behave according to some well-defined notion of effectiveness" (1990).

The desirable outcome of a well-reasoned philosophy is to produce an effective pedagogy, where pedagogy is not synonymous with method or technique. Pedagogy includes everything a teacher is and does when teaching and getting ready to teach. Methods and techniques are narrow and specific while one's pedagogy is more holistic. A technique might be found effective by one particular teacher, for a particular group of students, to teach a certain specific content. A good pedagogy *selects* what is appropriate and is not wedded to a method, no matter how innovative or popular.

I will return to Brookfield for the last word on relating philosophy to what we do in the classroom. "Without a personal organizing vision we are rudderless vessels tossed around on the waves and currents of whatever political whims and fashions are prevalent at the time" (1990). An effective teacher will neither embrace nor disdain teaching methods because they are either innovative or traditional. An informed eclecticism fits well into a good philosophy of teaching.

Can we then expect good teaching to produce an educated student? Well, not always. Education is a word so variously used that it more often elicits a feeling than a clear concept. The first sentence in Barzun's seminal book *Begin Here* is, "Forget education." The rationale for this shocking opening is made clear almost immediately. Educating is not something that one person can do, and education is not something that any person or institution can give to a student. Definable activities of individuals are learning (on the part of students) and teaching (on the part of teachers). Consistent with Barzun's admonition I will use the word *education* to mean *learning that has been facilitated by teaching*. This definition will, again, be expanded on in chapter 5. For now it is sufficient to understand that teaching and learning are each one-person activities. Education is what emerges when the two happen together.

THE BIOLOGICAL BASIS
OF LEARNING

When we come to know something, we
have performed an act that is as biological
as when we digest something.
            —Henry Plotkin

Learning, like teaching, tends to be perceived and talked about as a phe-nomenon so commonplace as to be irreducible. What it means would seem intuitively obvious. When learning is teased apart and analyzed, the expo-sition will almost certainly use language more complex and less intuitive than the thing under scrutiny. "Understanding," "comprehension," "reflec-tive integration," and "conceptualization" don't seem to add all that much to the original. Learning seems to be one of those things about which we can truly say, "I know it when I see it."

That said, it remains true that a teacher who sets out to encourage or facilitate learning in a student would do a better job of it if she or he knew not just how the desired product will look at the end, but how it got to be that way. To do a good job of teaching it would help to have some notion of what's actually happening when learning is taking place.

Until fairly recently there was no mechanical explanation or model to even talk about. The current exhilarating resurgence of interest in the mind and consciousness, however, is having unexpected results. Attempts to produce computers that think seem to have had as their most exciting effect a renewed interest in the real brain. The work of Edelman (1989),

Changeux (1985), Searle (1992), Flanagan (1991), Pinker (1997), and many others illustrates thinking about the mind that is not just new but adventuresome.

What the mind is we'll leave to the philosophers, but few would argue with the claim that we think with our brains. What thinking actually is I seriously doubt we will ever know, but none of it gets done without a brain, so I would like to begin our consideration of thinking and learning by considering them as biological processes.

The neurons in the embryonic brain are crudely programmed by developmental genes to divide and spread out in rough patterns until there are a hundred billion of them, more or less, organized in clumps and layers so that when we are born, to a first approximation, all human brains look much alike. Isolated neurons, however, cannot do much on their own, and the ability of the brain to engage and make sense of the world is a function of connections between neurons. In the normal adult, these connections are both numerous and intricate (on average, one neuron has a thousand connections to other neurons). Neurons connect to other neurons by budding cellular projections that grow into long slender extensions called axons. When an axon comes in contact with another appropriate neuron, a junction, or synapse, can develop. The number and significance of these connections can be inferred from the fact that the *number* of neurons in the large adult brain is no more than that in the newborn. The several-fold increase in brain size with increased age is due in part to the immense amount of axon budding and growth between cells, most of which occurs after birth. It is completely correct, then, to say that the brain develops as we mature. But it is critical that we understand that this is not a metaphorical development. Cells actually make and break connections with one another throughout our lives, even into old age.

The paths that signals take as they pass from one part of the brain to another is, to the nonspecialist, simply bewildering. They fan out, converge, loop back, re-enter the path from multiple sites and probably do much more that we don't know about yet. One outcome of this complex circuitry is the ability to detect a speeding tennis ball, anticipate its motion, chase it down, determine whether it has top spin or not, and whack it back to a predetermined spot, all in about two seconds. Other circuitry can design a computer program that beats its creator at chess.

The Importance of Experience

There are two points of significance here for teachers. First, it is the multiple connections between neurons that allow perception and thought, and not just the existence or the number of neurons. Second, it is experience and sensory interaction with the environment that promotes and stabilizes neural connections. There is good evidence that neurons bud, or send out new axons, continually. These new axons make connections with other neurons, but the connections, or synapses, are, initially, quite labile, meaning here that they easily regress if not used. New and weak synapses stabilize only if they have produced a useful path. Whether or not a synaptic sequence stabilizes is determined by the frequency with which that path is used. Even potentially useful neural pathways will, then, degenerate if not used. Genetics dictates the overall positioning of neurons. But in the thinking part of the brain genetics does not program the final "hard wiring" of the neural connections we find in the adult brain. These are largely the result of our experiences (Changeux 1985). How experiences stabilize neuron connections is just beginning to be understood, but that they do is no longer in question. One thing seems sure: mature neurons are still capable of budding and making new connections to other neurons and seem to make and stabilize these connections in response to repeated signals along a given path (Stevens 1993). One can imagine something like a rule that says, if a path is used repeatedly it must be important, so make it easy by increasing the probability that the signal will get through. Such a model is certainly consistent with common experience and the fact that both physical and mental activity get easier with practice.

A Theory of Learning

It is possible to make up interesting stories about learning based on neural budding and new connections stabilized by repeated use. A child, trying to make sense of the world, probably gets things wrong more often than not. Each attempt might use new connections that provide a representation of reality. The child's learning could be considered a matter of testing its representations against real world situations—experimenting, in other words. Several representations might be set up and tested until one works consistently. That pathway gets used repeatedly and becomes hard-wired—a preferred and stabilized path emerging from multiple synapses achieved through budding and made permanent through use. The genius of William James becomes apparent when it is noted that he intuitively understood this phenomenon in 1899, when neural physiology was in a relatively primitive stage. He said, "Our nervous systems have . . . *grown* to the way in which they have been exercised, just as a sheet of paper or a coat, once creased or folded, tends to fall forever afterward into the same identical folds" (James 1904).

Progress, in this scheme, is a matter of increasing neural connections with more and more re-entry loops and cross talk. Thus a child might master the concept of "more" before being able to distinguish between mass and dimension, leading, temporarily, to the erroneous conclusion that the mass of a fixed volume of liquid changes as its dimensions change. The child does much testing and many trial synapses are set up before a representation emerges that can accommodate a change in dimension that does not require a corresponding change in mass.

The point of this foray into biology is to show that learning makes the brain different than it was before, and permanently so. James said something nearly identical many years ago: "Things which we are quite unable definitely to recall have nevertheless impressed themselves, in some way, upon the structure of the mind. *We are different for having once learned them.* The resistances in our systems of brain-paths are altered." (1904, emphasis added.) Learning as brain-change, rather than brain-use, is an idea that can make people uneasy. Students in particular, on the few occasions when I have brought the matter up, are decidedly cool toward the idea of having their brains changed. For our purposes here I offer the hypothesis that the way you approach the job of teaching will depend on whether you perceive before you brains that may be forever modified in response to your efforts, or brains that are hard-wired and will simply be used to process the content material—something like wet, mushy computers.

Theory Affects Teaching

Both your presentation of material and your expectations with respect to student response will be influenced by how you perceive the learning brain in apposition to your own. Teachers, and new teachers in particular, are often impatient with students who struggle with the obvious. But the obvious is not always intrinsically so. What a teacher finds obvious might better be called *familiar*. Relationships of considerable complexity can become familiar through repeated experiences. In terms of brain circuitry, this would mean that a mental process had been repeated until multiple synapses had made one network of paths, or a mental state, the preferred one. To say that a mental process has been repeated does not mean that it is repeated exactly, the way one might repeat a long number to memorize it. More often mental circuitry gets "burned in," so to speak, when a circuit, possibly quite complex, is used repeatedly in a large variety of situations. We might consider this the neural explanation of abstracting—finding a familiar thread in a multiplicity of specific cases.

Daily immersion in a discipline, even a difficult one, involves representations being repeated until certain sets of synapses have been stabilized. The complex has become familiar. New students, even those with academic potential and good will, simply lack the brain circuitry that their teachers bring to the classroom. There is little danger in overestimating the intellectual potential of our students, but there is serious danger in overestimating the condition of their brains. If they do not catch on quickly to what appears to us obvious, it may be that we have confused the obvious with the familiar.

An example from mathematics will show how these considerations might affect teaching. Mention to a mathematician the highest possible or lowest possible of nearly anything, and you are likely to set off mental images unique to students of mathematics. Highest or lowest equates with maximum and minimum in their minds and that in turn conjures up images of complex curves and points on these curves where the tangent is horizontal. Simultaneously (and by now quite effortlessly) other pathways are firing away reviewing the fact that the slope of the tangent is the first derivative of the equation for the curve and the slope is equal to zero when the tangent is horizontal. These ideas are familiar to mathematicians but few of us would find them obvious. The new student may be as unfamiliar with photosynthesis, equilibrium, economics, or European history as the nonmathematician is with tangents and derivatives.

Seldom is anyone asked to teach at the college level in an area foreign to their experience. This means that for most of us most of the time, teaching involves rehearsing what is familiar to us. But without a philosophy that includes some consideration of brain biology we are likely to launch our familiar topics with the assumption that our students' brains are pretty much like our own, and need only new information. It should be clear by now that I find this a dangerous assumption. The familiarity we feel with our areas of expertise has come at a cost. The fitting together of facts and the strings of causality that now spring quickly to mind are the results of synaptic pathways that were once novel and experimental, but have, through repetition and reinforcement, become the preferred ones. Impulses moving over well-worn neural paths produce what we call familiarity. Even with the best of intentions students cannot produce in one pass the hard-wired circuitry that makes a concept familiar.

That these preferred neural paths are the result of considerable practice, and not some generic brain power, is evidenced by the discomfort we feel when required to consider matters that are well outside our experience. I have suggested elsewhere a policy that is in practice now on a few campuses: that faculty be required, periodically, to *take* a course from a colleague in a different discipline. The taking of a course does not mean attending a friendly faculty seminar. It means simply enrolling in a course, hunkering down with the undergrads, doing the assignments and taking the exams. On the few occasions that I have done this myself, my frustration was palpable. Asked to consider the opinions of Kant, Hume, or Wittgenstein on some topic, my database produced a few buzzwords, some vague associations and nothing more. It was discouraging to be below the median in preparedness. Surfing the Internet was not going to solve my problem. Certainly I had access to whatever I needed, but what I did not have was a brain with the required circuitry hard-wired through repeated use. Ideas lacked context. Reading was not a stroll through familiar terrain—more like bushwhacking through dense undergrowth.

Such encounters with the unfamiliar are chastening experiences. I certainly went back to my own familiar discipline with heightened empathy for the novice. I believe two important teacher attitudes emerge when we perceive our students as having brains of enormous potential, but unstructured with regard to our discipline. The first is that the activity that counts is going to be what goes on in the student's head, not the teacher's. A superb exposition of a complex topic is enormously satisfying to the speaker. The synapses are firing along all the preferred pathways and feedback loops are jostled just in time to tie together supporting arguments and inescapable conclusions. The brain is doing what it evolved to do and it rewards itself with an intense feeling of satisfaction. A teacher in this mode is like a concert pianist ripping flawlessly through a Beethoven sonata.

And what of the students (or the audience)? In the case of the pianist, someone in the audience who had heard the music many times, had perhaps played it herself, would experience something quite different from the first-time listener. New college students in a classroom are somewhat like the musically inexperienced at their first concert. Treated to a virtuoso teaching performance, the student response might be a great sense of awe— important, but well short of what is needed for learning to occur.

Certainly, during the grandest disquisition, what goes on in the heads of students is not comparable to what goes on in the head of the speaker. That fact has enormous import for the development of good pedagogy, and will figure largely in the treatment of that topic. For now I wish only to emphasize that a useful philosophy of teaching will attribute vastly more importance to the state of student brains, and what goes on there, than to the teacher's performance.

The second philosophical conclusion we might come to after considering student brains as having potential but limited synaptic structure, is the importance of repetition. The notion of repetition must be considered in conjunction with the fact that it is *student* neural networks that need conditioning. While it may be comforting and satisfying for a teacher to rehearse what she already knows, the only useful repetition from an educational point of view is that which goes on in the heads of students. This idea will likewise be revisited under pedagogy.

Preposterisms

Jacques Barzun (1991) coined the wonderful word "preposterism" for a large class of practices that arise, I believe, from the problem we have been considering: confusing the familiar with the obvious. Preposterous, from the Latin *prae* and *posterus,* meant, early on, that the natural order of things had been inverted—the cart-before-the-horse syndrome. Barzun uses it in connection with teaching to mean starting out where one should be ending up— a very old problem, noted as far back as Quintillian. If you have spent some years at your discipline, burning in the right synapses, and have arrived at a reasoned and convincing argument, the temptation to lay it on students on day one can be overwhelming. To do so might well constitute a case of preposterism. Many of us, when we were beginners, started our teaching at a level and a pace quite inappropriate for our students. It's an understandable mistake, because an unexamined philosophy of teaching probably sees it primarily as performance.

Teaching is easily perceived as a performance. You are the one; they are the many. You are the provider; they are the needy. They can be passive; you cannot. The butterflies most new teachers get on the first day indicate the teacher-centered mind-set they bring to the classroom. The result is a self-consciousness that is incompatible with good teaching. Preoccupation with performance overrides empathy with the student.

Preoccupation with performance prompts new teachers to cast about for a model. "How is this to be done?" is the obvious question. And we look to our own teachers for clues. Now and again this works well, but when it does it is the result of a rare combination of circumstances. We must have had one or more good teachers ourselves, *and* we must have been blessed with sufficient perceptivity and memory to understand and remember what they did, how they did it, and why it worked. The great irony here is that the best teaching draws attention *away* from the teacher. The very best teaching, like the very best writing, is often transparent. The better our teachers were, the more they directed our attention to things other than themselves. How does one emulate a pedagogy that by nature and design was trying to avoid our notice? Many of us in fact make a mediocre start of teaching, even as we try to emulate our own best teachers, because we failed to understand when we were students that these wonderful people were *not merely performing*, they were getting us to perform.

The performing teacher learns the content matter better and better because it is repeatedly rehearsed. More and more synapses become permanent, further strengthening already established circuits. A philosophy of teaching that incorporates some understanding of the biology of learning will prompt teachers young and old to shift the performing to the learners. It's in those brains that the synapses need to be made and reinforced.

These thoughts on brain development were instrumental in my decision to suggest somewhat rigorous definitions for *teaching, learning,* and *education.* If learning is indeed a matter of brain development—synapses stabilized through use—it becomes equally clear that it cannot be effected by anyone but the learner. Education, in most cases, is a noisy and public enterprise. But learning is essentially private, even when it takes place in a public and highly interactive environment. Things can be *studied* collectively, and profitably so, but they are nonetheless *learned* privately.

The Modular Brain

If learning is essentially personal and private, and it consists of stabilizing synapses through repeated use, it follows that learning can be externally encouraged, but only internally initiated. Such a statement, however, in no way relieves a teacher of serious responsibility and the effort that goes into effective classroom behavior. These ideas, in fact, point out clearly that good teaching entails a great deal more than abundant knowledge clearly articulated. The real goal of teaching is to persuade students to initiate their internal learning processes. My further remarks will all be premised on this conviction.

It must be remembered here that the brain is not a homogeneous mass of cells. Even the cortex, where so much of our awareness and thinking parts reside, has become organized into something like modules (Restak 1984). Our ability to hear and make sense of speech is remarkably localized in terms of the cell masses required for those functions. The same is true of our amazing capacity for abstracting, sorting out causality, and generalizing. Whoever first said that in some classrooms information moves from the teacher's notes into the students' notes without passing through the heads of either, understood intuitively that modules or regions of the brain can work relatively independently of one another. An experienced secretary at a keyboard demonstrates this convincingly. Such people can transcribe written notes flawlessly while carrying on a totally unrelated conversation with another party. When we exhort students, *"think* about what I'm *saying,"* we reveal that we believe that reflective concentration demands a very different brain activity than does decoding words.

This modular organization of the brain also has implications for pedagogy. The hearing and speaking modules of our students' brains have long since been hard-wired. It requires little effort on their part to hear what is said and to repeat what they heard. But making a new idea familiar means stabilizing labile synapses in a quite different part of the brain. As with all of us, students find that it takes little effort to "run through" well established brain circuits, but enormous effort, even momentary discomfort, to fire up previously unused regions of the brain and work those new synapses until they stabilize. Learning new things, in short, is strenuous. Students will avoid it if they can. Bruner (1968) has gone so far as to suggest that recalcitrant students actually "defend themselves" against this assault on their brains. Developing a pedagogy that can melt this icy resistance to learning may well involve setting up some new circuitry of our own.

We should not leave this topic without some consideration of the brain at various stages of human life. I mention this because of a common and distressing opinion often expressed by disheartened college professors. Some honestly believe, or profess to believe, that twenty-year-olds are well past the learning years and that if nothing of significance has been achieved by that age, very little more can be done than process them toward a diploma. There is just enough of a shred of truth there to make the point worth considering. It's sufficiently off the mark to make it a dangerous idea.

Shortly after birth the growth of axons and the establishment of synapses is, to use Changeux's word, "exuberant." The number of synapses is so large as to be multiply redundant. But these newly formed synapses are labile, meaning they can, and many will, break down, and the axon will regress or degenerate. Learning in the very young means using certain useful synapses from what amounts to a superabundance. Unused synapses degenerate. Changeux uses the expression "to learn is to eliminate" to characterize this process of stabilizing certain synapses from a redundant profusion.

To illustrate the point, linguists have found that the babbling of infants contains, collectively, all the phonemes encountered in any of the known languages. An infant, then, has the potential for developing facility in any language it grows up with, no matter the child's ethnic or genetic background. That same infant, when a young adult, finds some sounds in an unfamiliar language impossible to formulate, even though he made those sounds as an infant. The simultaneous or sequential movement of tongue, lips, throat muscles, and diaphragm necessary to make a specific sound involves the precise firing of an unknowable number of synapses in a "just right" pattern. These patterns, and many thousands more, were all there in all of us as infants. But it is only those that get used that stabilize and become part of our adult "hard wiring." The rest regress and with them the ability (without extraordinary effort) to speak foreign languages like a native.

What's true of phonemes is almost certainly true of learning in general. The profusion of redundant synapses make the potential for learning in the young far greater than is ever realized. In the young, the problem of learning is one of stabilizing synapses before they regress. Changeux's "to learn is to eliminate" can only apply, then, to children reared in a conducive environment. Without words, sights, sounds, and a variety of stimuli, most of that multiplicity of synapses would regress, and that unfortunate infant would grow into something only marginally human.

It is certainly true, then, that youth is the best time for learning. But it does not follow that learning comes to an end at some point, and that the resulting "hard-wired" brain is the one we will have for life. While the growth of axons is profligate during early development, it never completely stops until extreme old age—perhaps only at death. It's as if nature provided us an ample inheritance in our youth, but also a sort of trust fund to tide us over should we perchance squander our original windfall. Fanciful, of course, but it is true that axons bud and grow and make labile synapses throughout life, and it is true also, on ample evidence, that people can learn well into old age. The only hopeful position a college teacher can take is to believe that axons continue to bud in the heads of their students, that new and potentially useful synapses are forming, and that these synapses will, if everyone does the right things, stabilize and strengthen, and learning will take place.

I will propose later some reasons why pedagogy might stimulate students to do the right things and stabilize their useful synapses. For now we simply have to believe that twenty-year-olds can still learn, even those who have let that first synaptic inheritance dissipate through neglect.

3
LANGUAGE

Thinking is the mind talking to itself.
—*Plato*

If learning is students doing something to their brains, and teaching is trying to get them to do it, what is this something? At one level, what needs doing is fairly intuitive. The most junior assistant professor can sometimes be heard to say that what he wants to do in his courses is to teach students to think. That kind of declaration is not going to initiate a debate, or even much of a conversation. Older faculty usually mutter something like, "Um . . . yes," and rustle their newspapers. Now and then an old curmudgeon might unpack a bit of heavy irony and thank the junior for taking this innovative approach, reckoning that his success will relieve the rest of the faculty of a great burden. Why is it that experienced teachers struggle continually with the "thinking" problem while the newer faculty seem to find it an innovative approach that can be brought off through desire and good will?

Teaching Thinking

Certainly, thinking is what learning is all about. Teaching, however, is what teachers do, and the abiding question has always been what a teacher can do to make a student think. However enthusiastically they set out to teach thinking directly, most teachers soon come to realize that their own clear, logical thinking will not rub off magically onto their students.

But clear thinking remains the goal. If pedagogy is to have an influence it must, directly or indirectly, encourage and facilitate student thinking. The argument to be developed here is that a better approach is the indirect one. The idea that you can directly teach someone else to think is based on two assumptions: that the subject is initially incapable of thinking; and that once he has the knack he will be permanently empowered. I will argue that both of these assumptions are questionable.

Anyone who is not neurologically impaired to the point of unconsciousness not only can, but does think, and thinks a lot. Normal humans are all capable of even that special kind of thinking we prize so highly and call "critical." If we do not always see evidence for it, we would quite naturally wonder whether it is really going on. I would only argue that the operative word there is "evidence." Thinking, after all, cannot be observed directly. Sometimes a frozen stance and a distant look suggest that thinking is taking place, but there is no way to observe directly the actual thoughts anyone is having.

Language—The Window to the Mind

The real evidence for thought, clearly, is language. But there is a belief, widespread if not always articulated, that thought and language are more or less interchangeable. This assumption is best exemplified by the companion belief that students who cannot speak or write with some fluency are likewise impaired in their thinking ability. I held some version of this belief for many years. When students gave me the "I know it but I can't say it" line, I thundered back, "If you can't say it, then you *don't* know it." During all that time it never entered my mind that I might be wrong.

I'm considerably less sure of myself now. I have come to appreciate the work of the Russian psychologist Lev Vygotsky, who showed many years ago that pre-verbal children were doing a lot of thinking, some of it quite logical (see Kozulin 1990). Recent experiments have shown that even infants exhibit unusual interest, perhaps shock, when shown optical illusions that depict physically impossible events (Pinker 1997). These studies, widely spaced in time, present evidence that thought, of considerable subtlety, can precede the ability to articulate those thoughts. If thought and the capacity for articulating it are not intrinsically linked, then these must be separable talents that might or might not develop concurrently. The consequences here are significant. As teachers we can only deduce that a student is not thinking critically on the basis of evidence, but that evidence can only be some form of language use. If language use and thinking are separable talents, we may well be drawing an incorrect conclusion when we judge the inarticulate student to be deficient in critical thinking ability.

Vygotsky further demonstrated that language acquisition allows thought to become verbal and imposes a powerful organizing influence on it. Later, the work of Parry, Luria, Havelock, and Ong (reported in Ong 1982) showed that the invention of writing had an equally powerful influence on speech and even the way people think.

The intent here is to show that language—spoken, signed, or written—is the only way we can detect thought. When we say students can't think we are making tacit assumptions that their language skills are adequate, and that the students, out of spite or laziness, are not engaging their mental apparatus. A more defensible and hopeful model would be the belief that the power of thought pre-exists and that it becomes organized, explicit, and detectable through language, and only through language. This model is a hopeful one because language facility can be learned, improved, and taught. A teacher attempting the converse—teaching thinking skills to students who can't deal with language—would be at a loss as to how to start or how to measure success.

The studies and observations referred to above have led me, at last, to look upon the apparently indifferent student with less pique and more empathy. I now ask myself whether she is really indifferent, lazy, or recalcitrant—might it be that she only reads, writes, and speaks poorly?

These are not novel ideas. Readers who know Postman and Weingartner's (1969) quirky and provocative book, *Teaching As A Subversive Activity*, will have noted the chapter titled "Learning Is Languaging." "Languaging," when you get used to it, is a wonderful and evocative word. It serves as a kind of connecting rod between the separate activities of teaching and learning. I can learn by languaging myself, and teach by languaging someone else. This book is about teaching, but a great deal of what good teaching is, I now believe, is the inculcation of the language of the particular disciplines. William James was aware of this when he said, "Verbal material is, on the whole, the handiest and most useful material in which thinking can be carried on. Abstract conceptions are far and away the most economical instruments of thought, and abstract conceptions are fixed and incarnated for us in words" (James 1904).

Literacy

It hardly needs saying that language must mean more than vocabulary and syntax. College freshmen can be remarkably adept at storing strings of words in their heads—almost as good as the little tape recorders they sometimes carry about. They can and will learn the definitions of any term you require, or lists of the causes for various phenomena. But if a tape recorder can replay the desired words with perfect fidelity, then clearly the words themselves are no proof of any thought having taken place. Language here must mean considerably more than word storage.

We detect language facility through speech and writing, and the two are clearly related. However, just as articulation does not necessarily follow thought, writing does not flow spontaneously from speech. The capacity for using and understanding the spoken word is clearly a genetic endowment and normal humans raised in any social environment learn to understand and speak the common language. The same cannot be said for reading and writing. Reading and writing might well be called unnatural activities, in that they require so much effort and specific instruction. But reading and writing (literacy) have had an unexpected effect on the way people think, and that fact severely aggravates the problem of relating thought to language.

Writing is a technology that has had a profound effect on the way we use language, and as Ong (1982) and others argue, was probably responsible for changes in the way people think as well. Oral cultures do not use the syllogistic speech patterns common in literate cultures. In fact, oral cultures have little use for abstracting and generalizing. They are comfortable only with the specific and the particular. "We do not speak of things we have not seen," as one of Luria's illiterate subjects put it (Ong 1982). In a contemporary school setting, a person reared in a purely oral culture would be found deficient in critical thinking skills, no matter how well he spoke the language, or how successful he had been in his native society. Language in literate cultures is expected to demonstrate causality, generalization, and logic.

Secondary Orality

If you teach in a typical college you will discover that new college students are not, in fact, particularly literate. Whatever their thinking powers are, they struggle mightily to put those thoughts into words or to extract the intent in someone else's words. Should you try to engage them in discussion on the content of a course, you will find that their speech is likewise labored. In fact, the halting, labored speech characteristic of many classroom recitations contrasts sharply with the facile chatter one hears everywhere else. But there might be no real paradox here. If Ong was correct in his ominous suggestion that contemporary culture's reduced demands for literacy might be precipitating a gradual drift into a kind of "secondary orality," then the "language of the street" may come to resemble that of oral cultures and therefore struggle to cope with the literate demands of the classroom. As Ong and others have noted, literacy introduced an abstract, inductive, and syllogistic way of thinking. In highly literate cultures speech itself came to resemble writing because that was the best way to transmit logical thinking. Speech in oral cultures is quite different. It has been described as "performance" oriented—intended to affect the hearer in some way. It might be argued that the speech of an oral culture serves that culture's needs, but that would be true only because those needs are circumscribed by the limitations of the language.

To cope with the complex problem suggested above, many colleges are pouring resources into remedial language skills courses. *Skill* is a word I'm a bit skittish about, probably because it is so frequently used in educational matters to indicate something generic and adaptable. But I think it can be properly and usefully applied to some aspects of language use. There is, for example, a generic skill that most of us take for granted, but which is a learned skill and can probably be taught. And that is the ability to note with particular care the effect that the ordering and position of some very common and innocuous looking words have on the meaning imbedded in discourse. Some word clusters, even when devoid of any specialized or esoteric vocabulary, require a practiced deciphering skill to extract the meaning put there by the speaker or writer. The expression, "but not if," for example, cannot be misunderstood, glossed over, ignored, or mentally misplaced without grave consequence for meaning. Sentences with conditional modifiers demand not just alertness, but a certain skill in holding one idea in a kind of mental buffer until those modifiers have done their work on it, at which point it is "released" and becomes part of a complex concept. You can confuse almost anyone by laying on them a sentence with two negative clauses connected by *unless*. (This committee will not meet next week *unless* the subcommittee does not meet.) The point here might seem trivial, but Alan Cromer (1997) in his book, *Connected Knowledge*, notes repeatedly the difficulty college students have with *but, however, even,* and *only*. Healy (1990) also comments at considerable length on the importance of what she calls "function words" or "syntactic markers" such as *if, unless, because of, only after,* and so on. She concludes, somewhat glumly, that they are becoming obsolete among school children.

The ability spontaneously to decode language that contains subtle concepts is an acquired skill even if the subtlety lies in nothing more exotic than connectors and modifiers. The skill to generate such language must also be acquired and demands far greater effort. The language use teachers expect, and far too often take for granted, must in fact be developed through concentration and practice. We come then to the nub of this argument. We all want our students to think, and we would like to believe that our teaching will bring it about. But the thinking we want is usually that *concentration* noted above that happens while students are struggling with the *language*. The only way to force thought, then, is to force the struggle with language.

One element of a teacher's philosophy should be the belief that everything will get better, including thinking, as facility with language improves. Compared with "teaching them to think," this proposed language goal might seem somewhat bland. It does, however, have the merit of being both realistic and testable. Should the arguments proposed here have merit, teaching language development might effect the desired thinking goal, even if the actual mechanism has been enabling students to get at, unlock, and get out, what was in their heads. As to language development being a prosaic and less-than-astral-plane goal, I can only suggest that you hold judgment. As all who try it can attest, the challenge will surpass your expectations.

The Thinking Habit

Some pages back I said that there were two untenable assumptions behind the notion that one can teach students to think. The second of these is the implication that thinking is a generic skill, and once students acquire this skill they will have it once and for all—like riding a bicycle. If this were true, courses with titles like "critical thinking," would be an absolute and universal requirement for freshmen and the rest of us would, as our old curmudgeon observed, "be relieved of a great burden." Unhappily, critical thinking cannot be acquired in a once and for all manner. Critical thinking courses do exist on many campuses, and such courses have been thoroughly researched. Students in such courses are, at the end, better able to solve the problems encountered in that courses, but do no better or worse in subsequent work for having taken a course specifically designed to teach thinking. This observation has been noted by, among others, Derek Bok (1986), and Erickson and Strommer (1991) who said: "There is little evidence that generic courses or programs are successful in teaching thinking skills that transfer across subject-matter domains."

What can be developed, given good teaching, energy, and some luck, is not so much a *skill* in thinking, but the *habit* of thinking. The distinction is critical for someone about to teach. Acquiring a skill can take considerable initial effort and willingness to take risks. But the skill, if acquired at all, seems to "kick in" at some point—you go from inept to not bad over a short span of time. Anyone who has learned to do the butterfly stroke, or to skate backwards, will remember that magic moment when it felt right. Almost in a blink you seemed to acquire the basic skill, after which it could be honed to any desired level by practice. (I recognize here the difference between having a skill and being skillful at something. Being skillful assumes a certain level of competence beyond the simple ability to do a thing.) Contrast learning to swim with the habit of swimming an hour every day. The ability to do a thing is different from the inclination to do it routinely, out of habit.

Perhaps one aspect of our philosophy about teaching and learning should be the belief that students have the thinking skill, but not the thinking habit. What they need is practice. Language, on the other hand, might very well be a skill yet to be developed, at least at the level required for college work. I have come to believe this and for that reason am no longer exasperated by students who claim they know it but can't say it. A perfectly adequate goal of teaching would be to boost substantially the level of our students' literacy, broadly construed. Literacy promotes verbal thought, which, happily, can become a habit. Many of my thoughts on pedagogy are based on the premise that the thinking habit is supported by, indeed dependent on, considerable facility with language.

I believe my own breakthrough on this point came quite a few years back, during a period when I was convinced that I was teaching my students to think. In a course in biology, I had been generating multiple choice exams carefully designed to test critical thinking about bioenergetics, genetic expression and the like. I spent many hours designing questions that would distinguish various levels of comprehension. The questions, and the options for answering them, were crafted with great care to detect uncertainty and misunderstanding. Student scores produced the predicted bell-shaped curve and I was confident that I was doing fine. But one semester, on a whim I suppose, I added a final question: "On the back of this paper, outline and explain the sequence of events that would lead to death if a mammal were deprived of oxygen." I thought this a harmless diversion, an opportunity for students to use what they knew to tell an interesting little story. The actual outcome was a shock. As I read, paper after paper, dismay gave way to depression. No more than ten percent could write a minimally adequate response.

The request that they generate language that demonstrated biological knowledge seemed to disorient these students. The writing was childish, mostly incoherent, and either showed no evidence of the knowledge used on the first part of the exam, or blatantly contradicted it. The vast majority of them appeared to understand nothing when they were required to generate the language.

What I did not realize at that time, at least not at a functional level, is that multiple choice tests require, besides memory, a basic kind of thinking skill that even freshmen (perhaps *especially* freshmen) have developed to a useful level. The thinking needed might be complex, but it is circumscribed by the parameters of the single question at hand. Any complexities or subtleties of language needed have all been supplied by whoever wrote the question and the options for answering it. My so-called essay question was devastating because it required habits of mind and skill with language that, for most, had never been developed. Applying a known fact to a novel situation that requires that fact is a way of thinking that takes practice. Teachers think that way habitually, but most freshmen do not, at least not in matters of course content. Of equal or greater importance, my question necessitated language that illustrated linkages, logic, and causality. It was that demand in particular that waylaid the majority. It was almost as if the instruction to *write* obliterated what the multiple choice section had suggested that they knew. Typical answers were, "everything will die without oxygen," or, in a remarkable upending of causality, "animals need oxygen in order to breathe." I then began asking more open ended questions in class and found immediately that when it came to verbalizing consequential relationships, their speaking skills were no better developed than their writing skills.

Realistic Expectations

A teacher can enter the classroom, then, with severely misplaced expectations. Having spent many years in a highly literate environment, we tend to take a similar level of literacy in our students as a given. Many of them, on the other hand, have gotten along reasonably well without getting too entangled with the subtleties of the written word. Their use of language, resembling, as it does somewhat, that of oral cultures, lacks that quality of inventiveness that is a hallmark of literate speech. Rounding up the just-right words and stringing them together syntactically to transmit thought is, in fact, a formidable task. That most of us do it on the run, so to speak, is as much a testament to our facility with the language as to any exceptional skills in critical thinking.

One's philosophy of teaching and one's pedagogy influence one another in a kind of positive feedback loop. Our beliefs about students, our institutions, and even ourselves, can be soured should our pedagogy fail, or provide only frustration. By the same token, pedagogy will be lackluster at best if we start with negative feelings or beliefs about students and the whole business of teaching. On a happier note, an upbeat and well-considered philosophy and a successful pedagogy likewise reinforce one another in something of an upward spiral.

My intent in these reflections is to investigate ways to nudge both philosophy and pedagogy in at least small increments and in a positive direction. Inspiring and instructing young people to verbalize and articulate thought will likewise initiate a circle of positive feedback between thinking and language and send students off on their own spiral of lifelong learning.

4

TODAY'S FIRST-YEAR STUDENTS

So, if you are interested in teaching, do
not even expect the young to be like
yourself and the people you know.
                    —*Gilbert Highet*

For a variety of social and economic reasons, students are entering college
generally unprepared for what awaits them. Reduced performance expectations at the secondary level are just one of several influences that shape
today's freshmen. Cultural habits, for example, can change dramatically
within a lifetime. Grandparents don't quite know what to make of their
grandchildren; college teachers are equally perplexed with their young
charges. But Highet's quotation that opens this chapter is some fifty years
old, which suggests that young people have always been something other
than what their elders expect. If the goal of teaching is to educate, all teachers of college freshmen would do well to learn what they can about these
young people, their attributes, weaknesses, and habits of mind.

There is considerable good news to begin with. Virtually all new college
students have lost their reference group. They are now on someone else's
turf and for the moment are unsure of their companions in the same situation. They are alone in a crowd. This is good news. In general, at least at the
beginning, they will behave differently than they did a few months back in
their friendly high school. They are not likely, just yet, to slip into a state of
relaxed comfort. Jerome Bruner (1968) noted that "A child in a baseball

game behaves baseball; in the drugstore the same child behaves drugstore." He makes that point to emphasize that young people, as a result of a long period of conditioning, will quickly begin to "behave classroom" once they find themselves in that situation. Recently transplanted students, however, afford a teacher a wonderful opportunity to provide a fresh start. It's a good time to inculcate new habits before the old ones resurface.

Another bit of good news is that the nineteen-year-old is *not* just a four-teen-year-old five years later. The combined effects of getting to the end of the teens and being transported to a new environment can have a refreshing effect. Several people have told me, and others have agreed with the obser-vation, that they began to see their own children as people somewhere around age nine or ten. Five or six years later they are like strangers in the house, and somewhere around age twenty they become "the kids" again.

This might not be a common phenomenon, but it strikes a resonant chord with me. Having taught age groups from twenty-four years down to thirteen (and a brief stint with ten-year-olds), I also find that the twenty-year-old frequently resembles, in certain traits, the eleven-year-old more than the sixteen-year-old. These traits are subtle: how they interact with those older than themselves, what they laugh at—and how they laugh—their friendli-ness, their approachability, a certain amount of playfulness. No doubt I make too much of this. A few notable examples can commandeer one's attention. But it remains true that I find young college students a generally likable lot, and I always think of them as "the kids."

A Changing Population

But the news is not all good. At one time a college instructor might engage a class of first-year students as a select group of young people who were aware of their need for knowledge and practice in analysis and rhetoric, but pretty much primed and ready to go. College freshmen might be expected to have mastered the rudiments of algebra and trigonometry, to have demonstrated the ability to write passable prose, to have encountered, at least, a foreign language, to have developed the knack of reflective reading, and to be carry-ing in their heads a reasonable number of facts about the world, its geogra-phy, and the central elements of its history, its literature, music, and art. Are these expectations realistic today?

Well, much depends on where you find yourself. Institutions of higher learning are variable with respect to faculty, admission standards, resources, and their expectations of students. Eble (1983) describes a humorous taxonomic sorting of colleges and universities into "limbo, purgatory, and paradise." The simple truth is, the great majority of us teach somewhere other than in the handful of highly prestigious and highly selective institutions. The grunt work is going on in the less selective state universities and colleges, regional or branch campuses, private institutions, and community colleges. Something close to two million students start college each year and the great majority of them enter these more moderately selective schools. It's these young people that we need to learn something about because they are not as ready for college as their predecessors were.

Brains Under Construction

Typical college freshmen have had nineteen years to structure their brains, imbibe their culture, and discover their centers of satisfaction (at least a few of them). We are not dealing with a *tabula rasa*. It's far easier to teach a five-year-old (given the talent and skill to do it) than a nineteen-year-old. Five-year-olds have not yet hard-wired too many inappropriate synapses and they have a far larger number of redundant, labile synapses to play with and try out. Nineteen years of experience do not make the young adult brain easier to deal with.

But certainly these young people must have learned something during those nineteen years. They must be better prepared for college than a five-year-old. This is true. They have indeed learned a lot. Some of what they have learned, however, is counterproductive. Many will have habits, of mind and body, quite inappropriate for the task they are about to undertake. In the case of first-year students, a prominent element of teaching might be thought of as a reconstructing of the student mind. Making the difficult but necessary conceptual changes might involve something like demolition before construction can begin. Why this frightening metaphor?

First of all, college freshmen are, by and large, sick to death of school. Thirteen years is a long time by any standards, but for typical first-year college students it's 70 percent of their lives. Far too many see college simply as the last of the hurdles. At last there is light at the end of the tunnel. Four more years and it's all over. One day at a time, and so on. As teachers we need to appreciate a certain lack of enthusiasm here for matters of the mind.

There is nothing malicious in this, it's simply a matter of their extrapolating from their previous experiences.

Needless to say, not all young people have been soured on the whole idea of school. There are some exceptionally fine high schools that get their students hooked on learning and turn out knowledgeable, articulate, and endlessly curious graduates. But we're talking here about that big hump in the middle of the bell-shaped curve. Most first-year students are ill-prepared for the expectations of the average college professor. And if it is a case of inappropriate habits of mind, those particular synapses can be hard-wired and remarkably stable. It might take exceptional effort on their part, and ours, to bypass these established circuits and make progress.

Preconceived Ideas About School

It is not my intent to go into the details of why their prior schooling fails to prepare people for college. Hirsch (1996b) and many others have written at great length on typical pre-college schooling in America. Our concern here is the effects this schooling has on the young people we will be expected to educate. One major outcome is that they come to us with a mind set about school that is inappropriate for college work. And while they do come with considerable knowledge, that knowledge can be distressingly shallow.

Much of what students remember from high school has to do with a small number of key elements of the disciplines. Stock phrases stick in their heads: "supply and demand," "law of diminishing returns," "the Civil War was fought to abolish slavery," and so on. In algebra they remember selected operations, particularly "canceling," which seems to consist of crossing out any troublesome element in an equation if it happens to appear twice. These are the things that, right or wrong, for good or ill, have become hard-wired. These bits and pieces of information, shallow and fragmentary as they might be, provide the new college student with a certain level of confidence. This is not the good news it would appear to be. Their confidence stems from the mistaken belief that there is nothing really new here. After all, we've assigned them English. Well, they've *had* English every year for as long as they can remember. We give them mathematics—they've *had* mathematics. Chemistry? They've *had* that too. And so on for biology, physics, history, psychology, and the lot. As someone once noted, they have an "immunization" mentality about the disciplines. Once you've *had* something you're immune and it can't hurt you any more.

A young woman who registered for my introductory biology course displayed the immunization attitude to an amazing degree. After distributing the syllabus on the first day, I never saw this student again, until the day of the first scheduled exam, when she showed up, wrote what she could, and left. She was not seen again until the second exam when she once again appeared. This time I asked her why she was not coming to class. With a sincerely innocent smile she answered, "Oh, I had biology in high school." While this might be an extreme case in a behavioral sense, something like the same attitude is widespread among first-year students. It's part and parcel of a belief that college is a societally contrived annoyance designed to keep them warehoused for a few more years. Academically it's just more of the same.

So what of Elmore's (1996) "core of educational practice," that close interaction of student and teacher in classroom or lecture hall? What about Barzun's (1991) "first mature interplay of minds?" Well, we have to make that happen. But minds can only interplay by means of language. To repeat Postman and Weingartner's (1969) dictum, "learning is languaging."

A Problem of Communication

What then is the status of language in the case of new college students? While talking about the brain I noted the difference between the obvious and the familiar. This is a problematical area even when nothing but the most commonplace language is involved. Our greater experience and more extensive practice with the language allow us to decode a lot of meaning from a carefully constructed phrase, and to encode equally subtle content into our own speech. But what is obvious to us, again through familiarity, might be completely obscure to students. Or worse, it might mean the wrong thing because they have their private meanings for words. A simple example is the word *study*.

Anyone who has been through graduate school, done some original research, and written articles or books, has a clear and detailed idea of what it means to study a topic. It's not enough to recognize words, titles, or authors. Things must be learned so thoroughly that the probability of being tripped up by careless inaccuracies or approximations becomes vanishingly small. And so when we use the word *study* we intend our own robust meaning. When the college freshman hears *study* he understands something quite different.

The enormous difference between the teacher's and the students' perception of study can be illustrated by another personal example. Following a highly recommended and intuitively useful technique, I set a class of about forty students to work in groups of three or four. My intent was that they review the previous period's topics in preparation for a period of questioning and discussion. I gave my explanatory spiel about the efficacy of verbalizing ideas, hearing one's own and others' versions of what's important or how things work, and the benefits of writing and re-writing these versions until a clear and well-articulated explanation emerges. After some further cajoling on my part, they set about the mechanics of studying in small groups— all but one young man.

This student kept his back to the group and gazed absently and contentedly out the window. When I urged him to join the others he informed me that he "only *studied* for tests." It was said in total innocence, and with a smile, but also with a touch of that smugness young people reserve for occasions when they find it necessary to instruct grownups on the facts of life. What I was attempting here had to do with studying, and he already had that matter well in hand.

While his behavior was exceptional, the attitude toward study that he made explicit is widespread. Freshmen will often excuse themselves from highly attractive diversions because they "have a test *tomorrow.*" It's a rare student who will go off and study psychology, not because a quiz is coming up, but simply because psychology is getting ahead of her and she needs to catch up.

What most teachers mean by study would be the sort of thing we would do in preparation for giving a presentation at a professional meeting. Unless it was a talk that had been given several times before, it's hard to imagine that any of us would start organizing our thoughts only the night before. This *is* the mind set, however, of most first-year students in typical colleges and universities. Study, when there is no test in the offing, seems a very peculiar idea. What's the point?

The idea that the only reason for study is to pass tests might seem a peculiar one to teachers, but that conviction comes naturally to freshmen. They know about school, so they "know" about study. Bok (1986) has also noted that the very long period of schooling they have endured is more likely to have jaded young people than prepared them for this last bit of it. They are quite confident that they know how the school game is played. And *game* is a telling word.

The kind of misunderstanding precipitated by the word study is in fact a generic problem. As educated adults we expect a well-articulated idea to resonate in the head of a listener. But if the listener does not attend to syntactic subtleties, or imposes private meanings on words, what resonates might be wildly at odds with what we intended. Language is a particularly pressing problem in the education of freshmen.

School Versus Reality

One of the most obstinate notions that needs dislodging from the minds of new students is their conviction that school, including college, does not deal with real things. Taped on the office doors of college teachers around the country is a famous Doonesbury cartoon. A college instructor, trying only to shock his class into listening, is mouthing absolutely outrageous absurdities and blatantly contradictory assertions. He watches in despair as the students copy it all carefully into their notes. Students will, in truth, learn, and repeat faithfully, things that they would never use, or even consider plausible, in a real life situation. For many, school has come to represent a totally contrived and artificial system. It has, in other words, all of the required elements of a game.

No sensible person would believe that running across a certain chalked line with a ball under their arm has anything at all to do with survival, paying the bills, raising the kids, or making sense out of life. But we can all suspend our disbelief for a while, fall in with the completely arbitrary rules of football, and get caught up in it as a temporary diversion. It's debilitating to think that students enter college with similar attitudes, but the analogy is not terribly far off the mark. Convincing examples are those students in chemistry who can learn the complex relationships between temperature, heat content, and phase change, and still believe that, in the real world, hot water will freeze faster than cold. New students are quite prepared to play a game by any rules we lay down, but they do not take readily to mixing up "school facts" and their real beliefs. Doing so requires a conceptual change, an idea that will get considerable attention later in these pages.

As noted earlier, Bruner (1968) sees in some students the tactic of defending themselves in the face of new ideas. Nickerson, Perkins, and Smith (1985) have noted the same idea and suggest that "the real problem [the student] faces in such situations from his own point of view may be that of protecting himself." This is not a far-fetched notion. To change our minds at someone else's suggestion can be traumatic. It should not be surprising if students want to keep their comfortable synaptic pathways intact. To do so they will store disconcerting "facts" in the "school stuff" compartment where they will do no harm. A variation of this tactic is the cordoning off of school knowledge by individual disciplines and courses. History is history and philosophy is philosophy—the safest course of action is to keep them well isolated. New students actually take care to see that sociology does not slosh around and spill over into economics, and that biology doesn't get muddled up with psychology. The vaunted integrative learning we value so highly is just the thing that first-year students protect themselves against.

Transferability—Reality or Illusion

I believe the cordoning phenomenon goes a long way toward explaining the very marginal effect that skills courses have on beginning students. Professional educators write with some persistence about "transferable skills" in spite of widespread evidence that the whole notion might be illusory. Bok (1986) quoted the following from a National Academy of Science report: "Cognitive research confirms that knowledge and skills learned without conceptual understanding or functional application to problems are either forgotten or remain inert when needed in situations that differ from those in which they were acquired." Or, as noted by Nickerson et al. (1985):

> In summary, the accumulating evidence that skilled thinking is often more context bound than one might suppose cannot be ignored. This sounds a warning that efforts to teach very general know-how may not help students as much as one would like. It sounds another warning that people can easily deceive themselves about the generality of skills exercised by instruction. For instance, lessons thought to improve writing may only enhance short story narrative writing; lessons thought to improve reasoning may only facilitate formal deductive inference, and so on.

Nonetheless, there are courses in profusion on writing skills, critical thinking skills, and even learning skills. Many such courses in fact presume the very talent they would hope to develop—the willingness to integrate everything that is learned into a unified worldview of how things work. But, as suggested, new students find this a messy and dangerous course of action. We may believe that students are learning to think, and are practicing doing it, but most are simply studying for the exam.

The orientation course for new students, particularly the kind that intends to convert students to college level learning, is frequently subverted by the people it would help, because they see it as just another hurdle in this obstacle course called college. I sometimes use a small booklet with freshmen that I put together to demonstrate the expectations of college teachers and to show how these might be significantly different from what new college students are used to. To ensure that they would read it, I assigned sections of the book for study and paraphrasing until I felt that they grasped the meaning and intent of various chapters. What they wrote would suggest to most readers that they had a respectable understanding of the texts. But the lessons did not take in many cases. One unfortunate young man provided some evidence as to why. Well into the semester he found himself in clear danger of failing. In spite of doing well on the learning assignments, he seemed, as his colleagues might have said, clueless with regard to the course content, which was, again, biology. His situation had, in truth, become nearly hopeless. But, like so many his age, he figured this was an appropriate time to ask for help. In the course of our discussion it became clear that his study habits were pretty much those he had worked out in the sixth or seventh grade. When I reminded him of the suggestions he had studied, on college learning, his response crystallized the problem. With a wide-eyed look of genuine astonishment he said, "You mean we were supposed to *actually do* all the stuff in that book?"

To him, and a lot more like him, my assigning readings on college learning was just one more in a never-ending sequence of teacher peculiarities. They would learn whatever I asked but they were not about to change their minds about anything important, like how to get through school. Conceptual changes are upsetting and freshmen tend to protect themselves.

That Versus How

The transferability problem is further aggravated by the way new college students spontaneously categorize knowledge. They are generally content, and believe you should be, with having learned *that* something is true. Learning *how* something is done associates with music lessons and athletic practice, but hardly at all with the classroom. In the case reported above, the young man, and a discouraging number of others, had indeed learned some of the things that need to be done to learn well in college, but he was content with knowing *that* these things were so, in anticipation of my asking him to repeat them on a test. That anything learned in school books might be used to adjust one's behavior seemed to him strange indeed.

Expanding reality to include things heard, read, and talked about in school takes some getting used to. We probably cannot expect the majority of first-year students to get the hang of it immediately.

A Meeting of Cultures

Because the attitudes and habits of typical freshmen are at such odds with those of their teachers, new students suffer, literally, a cultural shock in their first-year of college. College, even allowing for some slippage here and there, is still primarily an adult culture. It revolves around the faculty and the grownup business of discovering and spreading knowledge. Without putting it in so many words, we think of students, certainly our predecessors did, as being invited to partake of, being initiated into, this adult culture of learning. The college president, or provost, appropriately festooned for the occasion, might express just this sentiment during orientation ceremonies. But these are primarily ceremonies, and most of those attentive young people in the audience hear only more "teacher talk"—part of the game called school.

To better appreciate the task ahead of us, we should reflect on the culture of the young. What they are when they come to us has been sculpted in about equal parts by genetics and environment. Anyone interested in pre-school and early school development would do well to read Jane Healy's nicely researched and very accessible book, *Endangered Minds* (1990). While Healy writes with a consistently upbeat voice, the overall picture that emerges is something less than hopeful. For a generation at least, young people have been entering school inexperienced in the kinds of mental engagement with adults that prepare a child for school, at least school as most teachers understand it. Without quoting here from what is an enormous array of sources, suffice it to say that the major deficit is in language use and language understanding.

If a child is lucky, a good school environment will compensate for her lack of prior involvement with the language and the resulting diminution in logical thought patterns. But few things are more variable in America than schooling. The unprepared are often simply accommodated, or subjected to alternative teaching methods, tracked as slow, or classified as having attention deficit disorder (ADD).

From the many reports on contemporary schooling in America, it would be clear to most readers that language development is ignored or very badly handled in far too many instances. It's not my intent to do a critique of secondary education, but new and experimental paradigms, programs, models, and innovations do seem to flow through the schools in waves, and it's nearly impossible to make any general statement about American schooling except that it is not producing what most people want of it. A common opinion is that expressed by Daniel Singal (1991):

> Beginning in the mid–1970s these students have been entering college so badly prepared that they have performed far below potential, often to the point of functional disability. We tend to assume that with their high aptitude for learning, they should be able to fend for themselves. However, the experience of the past fifteen years has proved decisively that they can't.

The effects of language deprivation persist and show up as characteristics of adolescent culture. Young people, for example, don't like long explanations. A thorough explanation of a reasonably complex phenomenon requires sentences with syntactical subtleties, and sometime several such sentences. Making sense of sophisticated language of this kind demands a lot of cross talk between modules on opposite sides of the brain as well as ongoing signals to and from the prefrontal region. If they have not had repeated use, the necessary axonal connections will not have been stabilized and hard-wired. To make sense of complex language, the unpracticed listener must make use of whatever labile connections are there. This can be done, no doubt, but it requires exceptional effort and most complain that it makes their head hurt. If you don't believe sending messages over unused synapses is stressful, try writing with the wrong hand for a while.

Quick, Fun, and Easy

Most of us, having struggled with them at length, are well aware of the difficulties lurking in our discipline. These are not contrived difficulties; they're intrinsic to any serious field of study. Our sincere expectations that beginning students make the effort to struggle with these difficulties will seem to them more like perversity, or gratuitous meanness. Those of us who teach freshmen are consistently criticized for "making it too hard" or for our inability to "make it easy." Young people have been continuously indoctrinated, from multiple sources, to believe that everything, including school, can be made quick, and fun, and easy.

Slipping Back into Orality

The culture young people come from is, as noted, more oral than literate. Few of their perceived needs demand reading or writing. Virtually all of their entertainment is visual or aural. Communication is verbal. Observers (Ong 1982, Healy 1990) note that what conversation takes place between teens has come to resemble that of purely oral cultures. It is highly idiosyncratic, often needs gesturing and body language to make intent known, and relies extensively on shared experiences or understanding between conversants.

Youth culture conversation is of such a type, and so ingrained by habit, that many freshmen have a painfully difficult time talking with faculty or any literate adult about anything except their personal feelings. As Healy notes: "The communication style of many adolescents, even when they are trying to cope with academic language, is often in the 'primitive' category. And because they seem to be less able to 'code-switch,' they are even more at odds with the adult world than teens of previous eras." "Why Johnny Can't Talk" might well be a fruitful topic for discussion among educators.

Personal Responsibility

Another characteristic of youth culture is its limited familiarity with the notion of consequence. At this writing, journalists are in a frenzy over the often tragic consequences of a common example, the refusal, or the inability, of so many college students to anticipate the consequences of excessive alcohol consumption. Automobiles provide equally horrific examples.

During the writing of this chapter several young people were interviewed on television because they were friends of the most recent single-car automobile fatality—this one the result of excessive speed. The common message they delivered was, "This could happen to anyone!" To these young people a car slamming into a stone wall at high speed was a matter of fate—not something caused, but something that just happens.

Such incidents represent extreme and grim examples of what is, on a less tragic level, a common trait. The causes for a diminished sense of consequence are debatable, but I suspect again that prior experience has much to do with it. Those life experiences include both the vicarious, in the form of movies and television, and the real. The real world of mass, momentum, friction, and impact force, and their effect on machines and bodies, is mostly theoretical to young minds. What they have actually "experienced," via the miracle of film, are thousands of auto wrecks, fires, falls, explosions, and gunshots that seem to do no one any harm, at least not anyone they identify with. At the same time they have grown up in a real world that is protective and forgiving. To many young people, consequences are theoretical.

Evidence for a history of overly protective caregivers is not hard to come by among college students. If they are dismissed by the dean for poor performance, or removed from athletics, the reaction is often shock and anger. The common question, "What do I have to do?" suggests a firm belief that *every* story can have a happy ending. *Something* can always be done, or *somebody* can make it all right again. Cleaning up after themselves is a habit too few young people bring to the college experience. There is something like an epidemic of "Acquired Helplessness Syndrome" throughout the freshman population. Few are inclined to anticipate, or to take responsibility for, the consequences of their actions. In the words of Healy, "Caretakers who are overly anxious about their responsibility for a child, who end up doing everything for him and 'picking up the pieces' of the problems he should clean up himself, are setting him up for later learning difficulties" (1990). The effect seen by teachers is a cohort not all that familiar with a sense of personal duty and obligation. The consequences for college learning are obvious.

Unready Minds: Underused Imaginations

Garrison Keillor invites us to listen to "A Prairie Home Companion" with the promise that the pictures will be "all in your head." And in the 1940s kids gathered around a radio each Saturday morning for "Let's Pretend," and let their imaginations loose, in full color, creating the most vivid visuals to match the stories they heard. Not many young people really *listen* to radio any more, certainly not to stories. Young boys no longer straddle old mops and tear off across fields, convinced that they are astride galloping steeds. Our students today come to us minimally experienced at imagining. Is this a problem?

In the first place it affects reading. The best books in any discipline tell good stories. They affect strongly only readers with vivid imaginations. Secondly, it takes a sense of make-believe to deal with the hypothetical. Arnold Arons (1990) saw as the first of several deficiencies among high school graduates the inability to cope with the hypothetico-deductive statement; if *this,* then *what?* It is the hypothetical part and not the deductive that causes trouble. Almost any statement a teacher makes that starts *if* or *assume,* and proceeds to describe an unreal (hypothetical) condition is going to either elicit an argument or sew confusion among a lot of new students. Doing hypothetico-deductive reasoning requires a suspension of disbelief—imagination. So simple a statement as "let X equal six chickens" will nonplus the student with no sense of make-believe. Part of our job will be to reinvigorate the imagination if we expect new students to understand arguments based on contingencies.

A Confusion of Goals

One hears a great deal about student goals. We need not spend time on the really big goals—good citizenship, happiness, and the rest. Everyone young and old agrees on those. Big goals seldom motivate day-to-day activities, however. The goals that prompt action operate on a time frame of semesters, months, or even days. A teacher's primary goal will probably be to instill understanding of, and appreciation for, whatever is being taught, and a clear perception of its ramifications in the overall scheme of things. Short-term goals will likely center around specific elements of the discipline: a circumscribed period of European history, the works of Mozart, selected elements from the periodic table, the major works of George Eliot, and so on.

So what of the students' medium and short-term goals? Maintaining a C+ average or better ranks high. Arranging next semester's schedule so that it is not marred by classes on Tuesday and Thursday, or at 8:00 A.M. on any day, is a big goal. Just getting through the current semester is a serious goal. The shortest of short-term goals is passing the tests.

All of which might sound cynical, but people who research this sort of thing concur in the main with this illustration. Academic matters are far down on the list of real goals young people have at the start of college. Schools of education that would have us frame our teaching around student goals seem to have little practical knowledge in these matters.

When we consider teachers' goals in light of the *real* goals of students, the whole thing looks like a disaster in the making. The point at the moment, however, is just to get as accurate a picture as possible of who it is we are about to interact with and how their attitudes compare with our own. What we eventually do as teachers will be largely determined by our perception of students' goals in light of our own.

Avoiding Simplistic Analyses

Understanding the new college student is a complex undertaking and we are often tempted to reduce it to something that is conceptually simpler to deal with. A colleague dropped by my office after a bad day and summed up his view of the matter with a sigh, "Words have no meaning for these people." That far-from-original observation is, in fact, a sort of diagnostic symptom of the whole freshman problem. But as a diagnosis it is too simplistic to be useful. That words appear not to register is just a result of the many aspects of youth culture mentioned above. Certainly young people can decode words, if they aren't too technical and don't come in big bunches. But beside the possibility that they might have private meanings for words, it is also true that they hear everything in context—in school. The meanings of school words, like the rules of a game, are arbitrary and irrelevant out of context.

This bizarre situation is not always appreciated. I have heard it suggested at an orientation planning meeting that students get a bad start in college because they don't know what's expected, so the solution is simply to tell them what's expected. That innovative idea came from a new member who couldn't know that the speech he was suggesting had been given every year for as long as anyone could remember, with no discernible effect.

You Can't Get There From Here

We seem to have gotten into a catch-22. How can you affect behavior with words when the listener believes the words have no relevance for behavior? This is the "know that" versus "know how" problem alluded to earlier. In professional jargon, unconverted students have "declarative knowledge," but not "procedural knowledge." John Dewey warned of this conundrum when he reminded us that students learn what they do, and not what we tell them. That his remark was over-interpreted and led, inadvertently so far as Dewey was concerned, to the long, muddled period of "progressive education," should not detract from its essential truth. Dewey realized that, for many students, words are just board pieces in the game called school.

Much remains to be said about how this catch-22 affects pedagogy. For now, the point, simply, is that we can't expect words alone to have much impact on new college students. Words heard in school have little bearing on reality. But for teachers, words are true symbols—place-markers for reality. Many believe that it is the human ability to posit symbolism on sounds and marks that clearly distinguishes us from other animals. Students who prefer to leave the symbolic aspect of language at the schoolhouse door present teachers with a daunting challenge. Jane Healy (1990) made the point fairly sharply: "We seem to be standing in the way of an avalanche of brains that are misfitted to our educational objectives."

This long, doleful litany might make it appear that the cause is lost before we start. This is far from the case. Those nineteen-year-old brains have lots of unused synapses, probably more than their elders. As Hirsch (1996) argues, it is our "intellectual capital" that puts us ahead of students, who in "raw processing ability, may far outshine [us]." If we can learn, so can they. The trick is to get them to do it. Some of them do, and the evidence is all around us in the form of those juniors and seniors who hang around all the time, picking our brains, looking for books, and generally indulging themselves in this wonderful new hobby called learning. It will take some thought and study to achieve it, but the goal is to transform shallow, indifferent freshmen into interested and curious young adults. That today's freshmen are different from those of twenty years ago does not mean that anything radical or innovative is required. It only means, as Jacques Barzun points out so eloquently, doing what is difficult (1991).

It can become a labor of love if we learn to look past their collection of bad habits and find the remnants of their childhood curiosity. As Highet said, it's not a question of faults, in the sense of ill will or malice. They are simply shallow and inexperienced—young. We might close, then, with another quotation from the estimable Highet: "The young are easily changed, therefore they like to pose as being immutable" (1966). Well, perhaps not quite "easily" any more, but change is still possible. And some of their resistance is indeed posing. Many young adults simply need permission to step out of the youth culture and into ours—permission and perhaps an explicit invitation. Lowman (1995) suggested that this concern is part and parcel of good teaching.

> Outstanding teachers have often expressed the sentiment that to be a great classroom instructor one must genuinely like college-age students and identify with their interests, both serious and foolish. Appreciating the emotional tasks facing students puts their sometimes inappropriate, immature, or even self-destructive, behavior into a perspective that makes it more tolerable.

Anderson (1992) also saw both the problem and an answer:

> Rare is the undergraduate who has the knowledge and understanding to appreciate the full range of intellect of a sixty-year-old genius. A university teacher with the right temperament does not find this distressing, and takes great pleasure and satisfaction from teaching young students.

But to get out of this catch-22, the invitation to the intellectual life must go beyond words. As teachers we have to do something, in or out of the classroom, that will initiate behavioral changes in students. That our words have real meaning and that the disciplines represent reality is something that students must discover. *Our* part in *their* discovery we call teaching. And as suggested here, the situation is fraught with difficulties, but far from hopeless. As Highet (1966) noted, it's easy to like young people and many of them respond eagerly to any sign of concern for their well-being.

5

TEACHING
AND PEDAGOGY

An impression which simply flows in at
the pupil's eyes or ears, and in no way
modifies his active life, is an impression
gone to waste.
—*William James*

Because the real goal of teaching is to elicit learning in someone else, it is clear that teaching and learning are closely linked. But nothing is gained by failing to see them as distinct activities carried on by different people. For that reason I have chosen to look at education in this chapter primarily from the point of view of the teacher. In the following chapter (chapter 6), I will look at education from the student perspective. It will be necessary here to expand on my peculiar definitions of teaching, learning, and education, and justify their use. And it is a good time to take up the matter of motivation.

Earlier I defined teaching as *any activity that has the conscious intention of, and potential for, facilitating learning in another.* This is an uncommon definition and many teachers, particularly those in departments of education, will find it unacceptable. The reasons are easily discerned. As defined here, teaching does not imply necessarily that any learning is going on. In fact, it does not even demand that anyone else be *present.* It is strongly held by a sizable fraction of school teachers that unless students are learning, whatever it is that the instructor is doing, it should not be called teaching. For my specific purposes here, I've formulated a more clinical definition that expressly and intentionally separates teaching from learning, but only for the purpose of emphasizing that they are activities carried out by different people. This definition allows us to discuss teaching as one person's conscious behavior. It does not, thereby, preclude degrees of quality. Teaching can range from the completely ineffective to outstanding.

We are concerned here with teaching that is effective, and there are two schools of thought about how anyone comes to be an effective teacher. One holds that it is pretty much a matter of good genes. Good teachers are born to the task, and anyone who isn't will never be very good at it. Certainly, one's intellectual endowment and temperament are significant factors in teaching, and these will be considered in due course. My emphasis, however, will lean toward the other school, the one that holds that good teaching is a matter of doing the right things under appropriate circumstances, and that doing the right things is something that can be learned. The debate will not be soon decided, but the genetic-trait school doesn't hold much hope for those of us who happen not to have gotten useful doses of the right genes. I can see hope only in the belief that teaching is a talent, where Barzun's definition of talent applies: "fair material properly trained" (1991). This more hopeful model is particularly useful in those very common instances when a teacher encounters several classes of differing preparedness or capacity. It is furthermore the only model in which a discussion of pedagogy makes sense. Pedagogy is primarily a matter of what a teacher does in a teaching environment. If teaching could not be improved substantially through coaching, study, and practice, there would be little point in discussing it.

Elmore (1996) clearly agrees with this position: "Few teachers are predisposed to teach in interesting ways." If Elmore is correct, then "becoming disposed" to teach well should be of greater concern to teachers than worrying about their "being predisposed" to do it.

It is possible for someone to have been born (predisposed) with just the right instincts and so teach very effectively right from the start. The vast majority of us, however, have to *become* disposed to teach effectively.

With a definition of teaching that has intent and potential as its essential elements, we can see that teaching would apply to someone writing a book that had the potential for instructing future readers. "All books try to teach" notes Highet (1966). Likewise, someone recording a demonstration on videotape would be teaching so long as that person's actions and speech are intentional and have the potential for instructing. Teaching, then, is something done *by* someone, and not *to* someone. In a stroke we avoid quibbling over teaching history versus teaching students. By agreeing that teaching is done by someone and not to someone, we can only say that what we teach is our discipline.

We will need, nevertheless, a further qualification. Defining teaching as actions that have only the potential for instructing or educating might be too expansive. Clearly some teaching, no matter how well intentioned, might simply be inappropriate for a particular group of students. Teaching, then, admits to degrees of effectiveness. When it is particularly effective we call it good teaching—teaching that has the intent and potential to instruct but is also especially appropriate for a particular group of learners.

Learning was defined, equally clinically, *as stabilizing through repeated use, certain appropriate and desirable synapses in the brain.* Again, if such a definition were proposed to a group of teachers in an auditorium, I have no doubt that someone would grab a microphone and inform the speaker, and to lusty applause, that, "Learning is a lot more than making synapses!" This is an understandable objection, because learning, even as here defined, is often accompanied by certain dramatic elements associated with motivation and satisfaction. Still, I will stick with my definition in these pages, because nothing is lost by separating, for purposes of discussion, the actual learning from any dramatic or emotional elements that might be associated with it.

One objection to thinking about learning in the reductive way defined here, is that it can't be seen happening. Every teacher enjoys the luminous, rapt gaze and gentle grin that suggest comprehension, or the almost coherent avalanche of words that says, "I understand, I understand!" But I maintain that a rational discussion of learning is precluded by confusing lyric manifestations with the real thing. To believe that we can see learning taking place is to be deluded. Learning, in this book, will mean mental changes whether or not accompanied by external manifestations.

Learning so defined does not require teaching, even by my broad definition of teaching. But without teaching of any sort, learning is limited entirely to discovery through personal experience. Learning without any kind of teaching means learning without reading, because most writing is intended to inform and so was done by someone teaching, even if that teaching was done many years ago. These definitions allow us to talk with some precision about teaching—what teachers do, and about learning—what students do.

And what of education? *Educare* is the Latin root and refers to the raising or rearing of a child. But *educare* itself has roots. It came from *e* (out) and *ducere* (to lead). To lead implies a leader *and* a follower. As Patrick Welsh (1992) notes: "It takes two to tango." And so it is that education is defined as *learning that has been facilitated by teaching.* This definition eliminates the colloquialism *self-educated person,* but at no loss to our discussion here. The person who became learned through reading had as teachers the people who wrote the books. Such a person is educated as surely as those who spent a lot of time in classrooms. As things stand, then, teaching can be done with or without learning. Learning can be done with or without teaching. Education requires both teaching and learning.

Is there, then, some method of teaching that guarantees learning? An equivalent question would be, "Can education be assured?" Clearly it cannot because people cannot be educated against their will. So the more useful question is one of probabilities. What kind of teaching is most likely to facilitate learning?

In addressing that question we need to stay focused on the fact that learning can only be self-initiated and not externally caused. Beyond having knowledge and information, and the ability to relate it, it would appear that the talent teachers need is the power to persuade. Assuming we know what it is we want our students to learn, the difficult task becomes convincing them that it is a good and satisfying thing to learn it. This idea is consistent with Dewey's dictum that students "learn what they do and not what we tell them" (1963). Teaching must involve telling, but learning will only start when something persuades students to engage their minds and do what it takes to learn.

The "persuading" I speak of is what we commonly call *motivating.* But what does that mean? It's the verb form, *to motivate,* that causes trouble, because motivating, like educating, is a two-person problem. To motivate is to incite or impel to some action. But that implies someone amenable to being incited. Motivating is a two-person activity. It cannot, in other words, be done *to* someone, without violence, unless that someone cooperates.

I prefer, then, to avoid the verb form altogether and concentrate on *motivation,* the noun. Motivation resides entirely in the person motivated. It can be inspired and encouraged by others, but cannot be given.

What then, does good teaching involve? I see the major elements as exposing, and inspiring. Neither of these is a simple act. If they are to be "led out," (*e ducere*) students need a clear picture of where they are, and where they ought to be. This demands exposition by the teacher. I should note here that I say "where they *ought* to be" with deliberation. Teachers should not back away from the notion that learning the rudiments of a discipline is in the students' best interest and that they therefore ought to do it. This idea is implied anytime we impose requirements on students. Teachers are engaged on the assumption that they are better qualified than students to determine what ought to be learned.

Telling students what they need to know is one thing; *doing* something that will inspire them to become motivated and actually learn is quite another. Some years back, motivation was not something college instructors needed to be unduly concerned with. Students' very presence in college implied some level of motivation, and parents, grades, curiosity and the like would carry them through. Today's freshmen, however, as suggested in the previous chapter, have come to expect education to be the work of the teacher. Unless we are willing to let them fail in large numbers, or, worse yet, pass them on whether they have learned anything or not, today's college instructors will have to become concerned with motivation. A reasonably ambitious goal for the teacher of today's freshmen would be to bring them to the state their predecessors were starting from a generation ago. Weingartner (1992), while specifically addressing mathematics, was noting a near universal problem:

> For the foreseeable future . . . the application of *future* high school standards to *present* undergraduate institutions creates a sufficiently formidable task. Present colleges, in other words, might be thought of as being obligated to engage in a kind of anticipatory remediation.

Jerome Bruner (1968) suggested that few students begin a course of study at a high level of readiness. He saw bringing students to the point of readiness as a significant part of teaching. Indeed, it would take little in the way of talent and effort to teach effectively if everyone came ready to learn what we have to offer. Our thoughts on pedagogy will have to include all of our teaching behaviors: bringing students to the point of readiness, presenting material, and persuading students to do their part—to learn. We will need to take a close look at what we say and do, how we say it and do it, what we request of students, how we react to their successes and failures, and, finally, something I will call *persona*—the "teacher image" we present—the entity students perceive and interact with. All these aspects of pedagogy have the same two goals: exposition of content and inspiring students to learn.

Breaking Down the Walls

If it is true that many freshmen enter college believing that all schooling is a make-believe world, they will be, from the outset, at cross purposes with those of their teachers who see things quite differently. Disabusing students of their view of schooling as a game-like contrivance is a high-priority goal. A pedagogy that is contrived, and therefore obvious, will only aggravate the problem. The great challenge here is to achieve a way of teaching that looks spontaneous and reactive, but which in fact is carefully designed. An early goal of pedagogy is to reconstruct reality for freshmen, to make subject content real and not just an element of the school game. Your discipline must be presented as a slice of reality, and certainly not as just another hurdle on the way to a diploma. If you believe these things to be true, and that belief shows in your teaching, you will have created the environment in which new students can gradually come to see history, biology, psychology, literature and the rest as reality, and not as various aspects of the school game.

Two Way Talk

General James A. Garfield, speaking at Williams College in 1871, gave the classic example of an ideal learning situation. He said, "Give me a log hut, with only a simple bench, Mark Hopkins on one end and I on the other" (Highet 1966). We can safely assume that the General would not have sat like a lump listening to a wise man rambling on. None of us, given that opportunity, would have failed to make known our own state of knowledge, or ignorance, or to ask questions, or to request amplification. Freshmen, however, would sooner die. Not many of them start out with the idea that their teachers in college have something valuable to offer them, and that they should go after it. Their *modus operandi* is to never attract attention to themselves, speak only when spoken to, and say as little as possible.

In the case of freshmen there is no question that the most painfully difficult part of my own teaching is getting them to talk to me. Getting one-word answers to trivia questions is not hard—they've been playing that game for years. Nor am I thinking of the garrulous extrovert who will inundate you with a flood of "like-y'know" word clusters. By talk I mean something that sounds literate, comes in sentences, and is germane to the topic at hand.

What has this to do with breaking down the barriers between school and reality? I believe literate conversation is effective in doing just that because it precludes students applying stock answers to stock questions—the essence of the game of school. When a student is required to talk about some topic of the course content for just twenty or thirty seconds, in clear English, and without a script, something desirable seems to happen. The sheer process of fusing personal, *real* language with school facts begins to chip away at the walls. Simply talking in an adult way about a real event has the effect of nudging that event out of the game world of school. The effect is very different from that of asking for lists of names or dates. In the latter case you find out what the student knows, in the former you find out what he is thinking.

Student-teacher discourse is such an essential component of pedagogy that I believe it should start on day one, and that several minutes of most periods should be spent having students tell the class in clear English what they know, or think, about some topic, or even what they are sure they don't know about it. According to Hirsch: "If . . . speaking and listening skills have been impoverished by growing up in a limited linguistic environment, no effort should be spared to enhance those foundational oral-aural skills as a prerequisite for further literacy skills" (1996). Getting students to talk is of the essence. Bringing if off, however, is a matter of the greatest delicacy.

Your insistence on a considered response, with at least two parts of speech, will not be taken by most freshmen in the heuristic sense it is intended. More likely it will be seen as university-sanctioned hazing and probably worthy of mention on their end-of-term evaluation reports. What we are about here is difficult because it involves learning, in the sense of using new and untried synapses. Worse yet, it means not using some old and very hard-wired neuronal paths. Students are well practiced in the art of question-answer, as they understand it. For them the game is set questions having set answers, and they will resist your efforts to deviate from the rules.

The average time a teacher waits for a response to a question in the typical classroom is about one second (Rowe 1987). Teachers all estimate it much higher than that, but when measured, it is one second or so. Dead silence in the classroom seems to be unbearable. Most teachers will do something if no response comes within one second. And like Pavlov's dogs, students quickly learn that the embarrassment of ignorance can only last a second or so, after which the desired answer will be given or the spotlight will focus on someone else.

Mary Budd Rowe's extensive research on "wait times," suggests that waiting three seconds after asking for a student response produces a response more frequently than after waiting one second or less. She also found that waiting another three seconds at the end of a student response encouraged elaboration, extended explanation, and contributions from other students (1987). My experience bears out the findings of these detailed studies, including the fact that being stone quiet for three seconds in both situations is decidedly difficult to do and demands discipline and practice.

The pedagogy suggested here is intended to establish new response patterns and discourage students' ingrained defensive responses. Except in cases of obvious emotional duress, I tend to not let a student off the hook until something intelligible has been said. At the beginning this might necessitate a great deal of coaching—a powerful and most useful technique. In the case of a student who seems incapable of saying anything about anything, the prompt, "Would you say that. . . . ?" usually elicits a relieved, "Yeah!" At this point the student can be asked to paraphrase whatever it was that you suggested. If he makes a valiant attempt, don't spare the praise. There is no greater favor you can do beginning freshmen than convincing them that talking to the teacher in reasonably clear prose is a very good thing.

What I have just described might take several minutes of class time and would seem to involve only one student. There is a simple device that will keep the rest alert. When talking to one student, put as much space between that student and yourself as the room will allow. This forces the two of you to speak to the class as an audience. The audience will pay much closer attention to these interchanges than if you were standing near the person talking or being coached. Also, putting physical distance between yourself and the student makes the whole thing seem less personal.

Dialogue with individual students eats up time, and some teachers don't make use of it for that reason. But it is not necessary to talk with a great number of students to have the desired effect. Calling for responses from just three students a day will take only five or six minutes or so at the beginning of each period. It's a painful and difficult process at first and it takes real resolve to keep at it day after day. But the effects can be quite remarkable. My experience has been that those students not in the limelight pay closer attention to what's going on than if I were lecturing. "That might have been me" is going through a lot of heads, and if the teacher is diligent, they all know that tomorrow, or the next minute, they might indeed be the center of attention. That prospect tends to focus the mind.

An alternative to asking direct questions is to start a class period by asking a student to review briefly the important ideas from the pervious period. "Tell me something true and interesting that was discussed last period." Students will always try to divert your attention with some well-rehearsed response, "What?" or "Would you repeat the question?" or "I don't know" and so on. But by sticking with one student, and by encouraging, coaching, having her start over, and then by praising a final coherent sentence, I signal to everyone that I'm not playing the game—at least not the one they are familiar with.

As noted, the rest of the group seems to pay close attention to these exchanges. Usually the third or fourth person called on has caught on and is willing to do whatever it takes to minimize this badgering, even if that means speaking standard English. If a teacher has the stamina to keep at it, three students a day, every day, something quite unusual will happen. A lot of students will start coming to class "prepared." Once it is clear that a few well-chosen sentences on the topic is all that it takes, many, and in some cases most, prefer to come in ready to talk. Still, coaching their speech may be necessary for some time. According to Healy (1990): "They often remain silent because they can't get their curiosity into words."

In talking about pedagogy I have intentionally started with a device that is probably the most stressful for student and teacher alike. I do so for two reasons. It exemplifies, first, that real learning, being the use of not-yet-stabilized synapses, is intrinsically taxing. It cannot be made quick, and fun, and easy. Secondly, adult conversation is one of the most effective ways to force the struggle with language, a goal I consider primary. Eliciting coherent speech, as well as writing, will figure largely in most aspects of effective teaching.

Teaching as "Giving Notes"

The expository aspect of teaching, telling students what they need to know, would seem to be the easy part, or at least straightforward. It's highly unlikely that a college professor would be unsure of the critical elements of the discipline—those things that really should be known. It might seem a simple matter of transferring knowledge from one who has it to those who do not. But we must remember Dewey's warning: They don't learn what we tell them, they learn what they do (1963). We might modify that slightly in view of contemporary notions about learning, and say that what they learn is what they do with their brains. This point was missed by the early progressives who perceived "doing" as physical activity. The effects of this misunderstanding linger to this day in the misuse of exploratives, research projects, role playing, and other potentially useful techniques. All of these activities do have the intent to educate. But because learning is brain change and cannot be seen as it happens, it is altogether possible that a major effect of much of this activity is to distract or entertain, unless it incorporates the essential elements of learning. Meyers and Jones (1993), in *Promoting Active Learning*, are persistent in pointing out that what students are doing physically is not the important element. What they find to be the essential elements in active learning are, "talking and listening, writing, reading, and reflecting."

Which brings us to the crux of the problem inherent in the expository part of teaching. Somehow we must provide discussions, assignments, and other activities that *cannot be carried out without reflective thought about the content*. Designing such activities and testing for their effectiveness demands reflection and careful planning. Anything that students can do using well-conditioned, hard-wired old synapses will almost certainly be done that way. What they can do using old neural pathways will indeed be easy, but it will not cause learning. For these reasons I am a little suspicious of any writer or speaker who has designed a way to make learning easy. When the brain is doing easy things it is merely re-running signals through old and well-worn neural paths. By definition this is not learning. If, on the other hand, a young person is running signals through relatively unused pathways she must be exerting considerable effort (recall the difficulty of writing with the wrong hand). She may find it satisfying, or even enjoyable (the brain is designed, so to speak, to do this sort of thing), but it is never entirely comfortable. When a mental process is easy, it is either trivial or needs only previously well-stabilized synapses. Such processes certainly qualify as brain use, but not as learning. Brain use then, is quite a bit different from brain change, and it is the latter we are trying to elicit.

So what does this tell us about exposition, the actual relating of those facts, concepts, and relationships we believe to be important? Certainly it does not mean that we try to make learning difficult. As suggested before, most disciplines, at the college level, provide sufficient difficulty in and of themselves. It is not a question of making a subject difficult, but more one of accepting the fact that learning it is going to be difficult for most students. Teachers err, I believe, if they pretend that what is by nature difficult can be made easy through clever pedagogy. Any subject can be made easy by trivializing it, but doing so only perpetuates the superficiality and shallowness that we are supposed to be eliminating.

Our intent, then, is to get the elements of our discipline to pass through new synapses. It follows that the difficult work of organizing, abstracting, and relating is better done by students than the teacher. For this reason I personally do not think it a good idea that a teacher produce and provide a detailed outline or set of class notes for students. The temptation to do so can be overwhelming, and many teachers firmly believe it to be a good technique. This is not surprising because getting new students to organize their own thinking and generate useful notes on readings or discussions can be so frustrating and time consuming that all but the most stalwart will be tempted to do all of this brain work themselves and simply pass it out or project it on a screen. The real result of that approach is that the teacher rehearses one more time what he already knows and the students miss an opportunity to struggle with the language. Eble was quite clear on this point:

> Teachers should feel somewhat uneasy if all the things they deal with come out in neat lists, outlines, or classifications. Teachers may take some advantage of the ephemeral, oral form of teaching, of its immediate presentation before students, to leave some things uncounted and unclassified. Students, after all, should be involved in the process of defining, relating, and analyzing their subject to give it order (1972).

The picture that should be emerging is that teachers do a disservice to students by trying to make the difficult appear easy. Rather than providing students with a complete set of notes, or an annotated outline, we should be coaching them and encouraging them to develop the habit of outlining and organizing for themselves, through practice. These are valuable talents in that they constitute procedural and not just declarative knowledge. Efforts to develop these habits of mind will not be immediately appreciated by freshmen. They expect you to provide all that is necessary, and only what is necessary, to pass the test. Providing more than is necessary is almost as bad as not providing enough. Some freshmen consider it a terrible waste if they perchance learn something that does not appear on a test.

Students' perception of our job is made clear by the expression they use to indicate a teacher teaching—they call it "giving notes." Being able to detect just when a teacher is giving notes and when he isn't is one skill that freshmen develop early on. The click of chalk on the board says that notes are being given. The announcement that *three* causes, or *five* effects are about to follow is a clear sign. Notes are not being given when the VCR is playing a tape, or when pages from the textbook are being projected on the overhead, or when the teacher is pacing the floor and telling an interesting story.

As noted earlier, most freshmen have their own very firm ideas about study—something done just before a test. Study is done by something known as "going over the notes." Even if they do not use them optimally, one thing new college students all seem to imbibe is the value of "the notes." And it is not so much "their" notes as "the" notes. For freshmen, a good teacher is one who "gives good notes," and so all students' notes should be nearly identical. Freshmen love teachers who give good notes, because missing a class is easily made up by getting the notes from someone. For some students these notes take on a nearly mystical quality. They would not think of modifying them, or making changes in what has been "given." Mixing their own comments on discussions or reading into the official notes is considered dangerous indeed.

One great kindness teachers could do freshmen would be to convince them that notes are something they *make,* and not something they *take.* New students will not trust a set of notes that consists of *their own understanding* of some topic. But that is exactly what we their teachers do when trying to make sense of something new. If it works for us it should work for them. Is there something teachers can do to get students out of the stenographic mode and into the habit of using their note books as real learning tools? Like so much of useful pedagogy, it means trying to change old habits, and that entails persistent effort.

To get students to make serious and useful notes, notes that are the result of their thinking, we will probably have to become more involved in their note-making. One useful method combines coaching note-making with the daily short recitations described earlier. As noted then, some students begin to anticipate the recitation ordeal and come in prepared. A few have what might be called prepared statements that they read when called on. This is not really a subversion of the recitation process. I encourage it, in fact, because it means some reading and some thinking went on between class periods. Any writing that puts ideas into new words is going to help. Coaching, encouraging, and praising original language that summarizes or paraphrases cannot be recommended too highly. When one student can be gotten to produce a good analysis or summary, and the teacher makes a show of how accurate, or precise, or useful it is, other students will take an immediate interest. I have had bystanders—students who would otherwise never do anything to draw attention to themselves—raise a hand and ask that the analysis or summary be repeated.

I usually do not allow the repetition because that only encourages the other students to copy someone else's words. Instead, this is a good time to have a new group re-create the good summary rather than simply have someone repeat it verbatim. The point of spending class time in this way is to try to undo some of the bad habits and inappropriate ways of thinking about things that students bring to college. They dearly want to have "the truths," because the truths will get them through the tests. And "the notes" should have "the truths." They will abandon this tried and true formula with the greatest reluctance, and only if a teacher is steadfast and clear in letting it be know that the mere recitation of someone else's words will not be rewarded.

Typical note taking can be done at the fringes of consciousness. With practice, many people can learn to transcribe accurately while their conscious mind is occupied elsewhere. Do the following experiment sometime to see how focused a class is. Face the class and tell them, in a normal conversational tone, some crucially important information for understanding the day's content. Don't write it, and don't give any verbal clues that you are about to "give notes," just say it and watch the response. Experienced seniors will start writing quickly, maybe interrupt to slow you down, ask for examples, and in general mull it over. Most freshmen will simply stare back at you. In his book for students, *Study is Hard Work*, William Armstrong (1995) expends considerable effort trying to convince students of the difficulty and the importance of learning to listen. He is clearly a good observer. Most freshmen really hear very little of what you say.

Another device that affords excellent practice at listening, using language, and making notes, is to this time *tell them* that an important topic is coming up during the next ten minutes and they must know it well. Then *insist* that they put down their pencils and listen, and see that they do so. Encourage them to ask any questions they want during the exposition. Forbid them to write but tell them that *after* the presentation they will be required to make notes from memory. Follow through and provide a period of time during which they can confer with one another (and with you—this is not a test, it's a learning exercise), and make notes that they are satisfied with. This simple technique is almost guaranteed to generate a lot of talk.

As always, the sure way to get the mind engaged is to set it to struggling with language. When I find I'm facing blank stares after having made an important point, I look directly at one student and ask him to repeat what I have just said. The typical response is, "What?" suggesting a consciousness just arrived at from a distant place. Eventually someone will produce an accurate paraphrase. Question: "How many people wrote that important information in their notes?" This gets a few students' attention and after a short period of this kind of verbal engagement, more and more pencils are picked up and more and more minds become focused on the content.

Telling students how to make good class notes has no effect. What you tell them becomes declarative knowledge, but not procedural. Making good notes is a habit of the mind and, like all habits, comes only with repetition. It takes great patience to ask individual students, time and again, whether they have made notes on the gist of an argument or on a sequence of events. Freshmen, in fact, may resent being jostled out of a comfortable passivity. But you do them a favor nonetheless. With time and repeated reminders, they will begin listening to what you say, not just waiting for you to give notes.

Making a Definition

Defining technical terms provides a way to contrast making notes with taking notes. In philosophy it might be important to have a good grasp of "intentionality," or in chemistry, of "equilibrium." One approach, the one I consider less effective, is to tell students that these are important terms and then give them precise definitions. This would be giving notes, and doing so is simply playing their version of the school game. The method that forces a struggle with language is that endorsed by Arnold Arons (1990). He discovered years ago that starting with terms, and giving them pre-formulated definitions, is quite backwards. He urges teachers to describe phenomena and processes in sufficient detail, and with enough examples and questioning and answering that this sliver of content may be well understood. Then, he says, give "it" a name. In his words, "idea first, name last."

If you have never done so, I'm convinced that you will tell the story of "intentionality," "equilibrium," "glycolysis," "economy of scale," or "iambic pentameter" in a more interesting and imaginative way if you hold off using the technical term until the end. The improvement in student attention and retention can be remarkable.

This method has an added advantage. Once the thing has been thoroughly described and discussed, and the technical term given, the teacher can then ask for a student-derived definition of that term. This is a difficult thing to do and involves a great deal of brain work and struggling with the language. Few freshmen know the form of a good definition or that it has two parts—category and distinguishing characteristics. They almost universally begin a definition with, "that's when. . . ." Giving students practice at condensing a long and involved description into a definition is one of the better things we can do for them.

The Paraphrase

Still more demanding than formulating a definition from scratch, is the production of a *paraphrase*. There is probably no better way to learn content, from a text, a lecture, or a discussion, than to paraphrase the content in writing, provided the paraphrase is of a certain kind. Students usually think of paraphrasing as simply saying the same thing using slightly different words. Given the task of paraphrasing a short essay, without further instruction, most will rewrite each sentence in succession. Done this way, paraphrasing is a mildly challenging word game, but the job can be done without any understanding of the original writer's intent.

The desired effect of a paraphrase is twofold: to understand the original intent and to demonstrate that understanding. This is learning at its best because underutilized synapses have to be strengthened through repeated readings and mental reconstruction. More mental struggling is required to come up with original language that says the same thing. The effective paraphrase forces thought and the struggle with language. Brief instructions for paraphrasing might be the following:

1.   Decode each sentence so that its intent is clear.

2.   Reflect on topical units, such as paragraphs, so that the argument, or the writer's views, are clear in your head.

3. Write what the author is saying, but use your own syntax and vocabulary.

This sounds easy in the telling, but it will take considerable time and effort to bring students to a point where they can write a paraphrase that has required thought on their part. At the beginning they confuse a paraphrase with a summary, or a review, or a condensation, or a simplification. But a true paraphrase is not an evaluation, or a reaction to a text, nor does it even need to be a condensation. Excellent scholars (A. R. Luria and Lev Vygotsky come to mind) can compress so much into a few words that an expository paraphrase might be two or three times as long as the original. Nor does the language need to be simpler. Someone with an ample vocabulary might well produce a paraphrase linguistically more complex than the original. What is essential to the good paraphrase is clear evidence that the original was well understood. And to test for understanding, the product, as least the first draft, is best written from memory—without referring to the original. Few freshmen reach this level without a great deal of practice and coaching. But those who do have acquired an invaluable learning skill.

There is a common theme that runs through the three pedagogical methods so far described: coached recitation, note making, and paraphrasing. Each of these demands *inventive* language. Language in itself does not provide evidence of thought. The recorded message you get when you dial the library is proof enough. Students can perform like answering machines almost as well as tape players can. But language that is inventive—word sequences never before uttered—will be either gibberish, or a demonstration that real thinking has taken place. All of the suggested methods are aimed at the inventive use of the language. A student cannot talk to a teacher in sentences, or make a useful set of notes, or paraphrase (as described), without having ideas sufficiently clear that they can be verbalized.

It should also be understood that the thought content of student recitation or writing need not be original or creative. It's highly unlikely that a freshman will come up with a truly original idea about psychology, economics, or chemistry. But an absolutely original sentence that relates a known fact or logical argument is about the best proof we have of understanding.

In subsequent chapters other expository aspects of teaching, such as writing, examinations, and technologies will be considered. The intent here is to concentrate on those aspects of pedagogy that are most likely to force *verbal thought*. It is repeated verbal thought that stabilizes synapses, promotes long term memory, and causes learning.

It is also worth repeating that inventive language—spoken or written—chips away at that wall that separates academic matters from students' idea of reality. The recitation of predetermined lists or packaged definitions will only reinforce the game mentality that freshmen bring to college.

The Lecture

Students cannot be expected to invent language that makes any sense without some information to draw on, what Hirsch (1996) calls "intellectual capital." How do they get it? The expository aspect of teaching is of great importance here, more I believe than many give credit (see however Stunkel 1998). Textbooks have more raw and accurate information than most teachers carry in their heads, but textbooks make for dull reading. Far too many are just badly written, and the format, in some cases, seems almost designed to distract from the information they contain. In spite of the many witticisms to the contrary ("the sage on the stage" and the like), a major function of teaching is, and will remain so in the future, talking to students. Everything else (except the diploma, of course) they can get without paying tuition.

It is here that we must distinguish between teaching and good teaching. Someone reading the textbook aloud could be said to be teaching in its basic sense. A few alert listeners might indeed learn something. As a group, however, our current clientele will profit little from that kind of teaching. What kinds of expository discourse and teacher behavior push teaching from the mundane to the good?

In the first place, the atmosphere should be different from what students have come to expect, otherwise they will quickly fall into their own accustomed patterns of behavior. There are some methods and techniques of presentation that will erode the "school" atmosphere. Breaking away from a methodical, strictly linear, and totally logical presentation of facts and arguments might make a course sufficiently different to get attention. There are alternatives to a strictly logical and linear presentation that are intuitively sensible and that I, and others find effective (see Stigler and Stevenson 1991). The first involves a kind of grown-up storytelling. Every discipline has people interacting with other people or things interacting with other things. Chemistry, economics, and even mathematics all have interesting stories behind the theories. Letting content unfold like a story can be effective because logic and rigorous causality are often best seen by hindsight. No one, for example, would read mystery stories if they were told logically. A logical telling would remove the mystery. In the mystery, the logic seems to explode out of the story, usually quite near the end. The large number of people who read mysteries suggests to me that good storytelling holds the attention, even while we are not quite sure what's really going on.

The second presentation method is closely allied with the notion of storytelling, and has been put to very good use in the field of physics. It involves a bit of playacting on the part of the teacher. The idea is to present some essential or well-known aspect of the discipline as if it were being discovered for the first time at that very moment. Teachers who use this tactic say that they rediscover the arguments or relationships as they present them. Lowman (1995) put this quite directly: "To be able to present material clearly, instructors must approach and organize their subject matter as if they too know little about it." Telling a story and rediscovery might be the same thing in some disciplines, or two sides of the same coin. Both have the same goal, keeping the mind of the listener in a slight state of tension—curious and therefore focused. There are also obvious similarities to the "idea first, word last" principle discussed above.

A valid criticism of the lecture as a way of presenting content is that very frequently it becomes the *only* method of presenting, or in the worst cases, the only classroom activity at all. There is one pedagogical device that is low risk, almost certainly improves learning in the classroom (and perhaps motivation to learn outside the classroom), and is welcomed by most students and tolerated by nearly all. It is simply a matter of interrupting the lecture after twenty minutes or so, for a five minute study/performance period. Even this simple-sounding suggestion needs planning and surveillance, however. Merely announcing a break will not do. If the performance part is to be a review, or recitation, or a two minute written quiz, the group needs some direction. The break might be to review the first part of the period in student groups of two or three, with the idea of coming up with a well-articulated statement of what was not clear, or what might need elaboration or illustration. Other times it might be to produce two- or three-sentence paraphrases of the first half of the period to be read and critiqued by other groups. If a one- or two-question quiz sheet has been prepared in advance, the performance, after the small-group study, becomes a matter of taking the quiz.

One good outcome of a mid-period quiz on the first half of a lecture or discussion is that there is time immediately after to ask several students to recite what they wrote. This usually initiates some discussion and questioning, because everyone wants to know if their particular understanding was on the mark or not. It also satisfies one need students express that is pedagogically sound—quick turnaround. Knowing as soon as possible whether they are correct or not in their thinking is reinforced if they are correct, or it will quickly dislodge wrong ideas if they are not. The importance students place on having their thinking either authenticated or corrected as soon as possible is thoroughly documented in Light's "Harvard Assessment Seminars" (1990) referred to previously.

The mid-period break can be done in six or seven minutes. For the teacher it provides highly useful information on how to use the last part of the period. If all went well, you know it's safe to push on. But you may find that little of what you intended actually stuck. Disheartening as that might be, it is important information that you are unlikely to get any other way. Paraphrasing or assigning illustrative reading might be in order.

I suggested previously that when it is appropriate to do the talking a teacher would do well to let the information unfold something like a mystery. Telling a good story, or pretending to be discovering what you already know, suggests a certain level of acting, and that brings up another long-debated question. Is good teaching more a matter of performance or of simply "being oneself?" My own opinion is that this is a poorly formed question. To answer one way or the other, and behave accordingly, is to deprive oneself of whatever benefits the other alternative might offer in a given situation. If the question must be answered, I would say, "whichever the circumstances demand." In other words, neither behavior is out of line or always to be avoided. I suspect that a teacher who resolutely behaved only one way or the other might become boring over time.

Teaching as Performing

I am of the opinion that most good teaching does have elements of performance. In some cases it might even be essential. Lowman (1995) allows the notion of performance to run freely throughout his book, *Mastering The Techniques of Teaching*. The alternative to performing is "being oneself." But consider the embarrassing possibility that one's "self" might not be all that attractive, interesting, or even effective in the classroom. What then? I believe the debate might cool if we differentiate, again, between just performing and good performing. In the United States, acting does carry a lightly pejorative aura. That might be because so many of our actors are so obviously acting that we end up observing them and not their performance. I suspect the reason that theater in the United Kingdom has such a sparkling reputation is that their actors perform so well you forget that it is a performance.

Clearly, any teacher who "did an act" as they say—like a stand-up comic—would be deserving of all the ridicule he might reap. On the other hand, if it's all a matter of personality, what do you do if yours doesn't quite measure up?

It is because of this quandary that I introduced the notion of a teaching *persona*. I ask you to consider the idea from the point of view of students. In the classroom students observe, and interact with, this entity they call the teacher. They might find her interesting, amusing, likable, or maybe none of those, but in all cases this "her" is the entity they perceive. What they perceive may or may not be the real personality of that teacher that they are judging. I would call the entity that they perceive the persona. How much of the persona is the true personality and how much can be attributed to performance is variable from case to case, and perhaps this is as it should be.

From time to time students can detect the difference, but without quite seeing the performance aspect. In their words, "she's different outside the classroom." What they have observed is someone who has developed a teaching persona that is noticeably at variance with her personality. When someone really steps into the role of teacher and becomes the persona, it's hard to tell what's real. I have known several teachers who were vibrant and engaging in the classroom while being subdued or even dour outside it. More commonly the persona development goes in the reverse direction, as when the faculty clown becomes a martinet in the classroom and scares the daylights out of everyone.

I would suggest, then, that there is little to be gained from fretting about one's personality and whether it's right for the classroom. Time is better spent looking for an acceptable classroom persona—one students will like, listen to, and learn for.

The Persona

The classroom persona is important because that's the entity that students encounter. How students feel about a teacher has, for good or bad, a powerful influence on how they listen, whether they work at the course content, and how much they learn. Older students, and particularly those in professional colleges, can be sufficiently motivated to make the teacher persona essentially irrelevant—they look past it. But freshmen simply learn better and learn more if they like their teachers, all else being equal. But that statement needs some explication. *Like* is an imprecise word in the mouths of inexperienced students. They don't always differentiate between liking a teacher and liking a course. Most freshmen would like a course that had easy tests and no writing assignments. This kind of liking spills over onto the teacher, no matter what else he is doing.

So what attitude should students have toward a good teacher, or toward the persona they interact with? Well, respect seems to be the time-honored word, and a great many teachers aspire to earning their students' respect, even if it comes at the cost of being disliked. For many years I associated the word *respect* with something cold, very impersonal, even artificial. Being disliked while being respected, whatever that meant, did not appeal to me. But then I heard someone define respect for parents and teachers as "that healthy combination of love and fear." That definition resonated. The word *combination* is key. It means some of each and *not* some amorphous thing somewhere in between. When one has respect in this sense, the love is quite real, but it never completely forgets that the person loved is in a position of authority and therefore power. If the exercise of that authority induces intimidation, that bit of fear is not abject, but tempered by a concomitant love for a caring person. I have no hesitation, then, in saying that highly effective teachers, or at least their personae, will be loved by their students, but with that tinge of uncertainty that's appropriate for dealing with authority.

To be respected in just this way would seem a worthwhile goal for any teacher. A teacher whose innate personality elicited this kind of respect is indeed fortunate. When it doesn't, some tweaking of the teaching persona might be in order.

Teacher Behavior

Take it as a given that freshmen will, initially, be more interested in you than what you are teaching. They don't want you to appear nervous. They don't want you to be so preoccupied with the subject that you forget they are there. They want you to love them. Happily there are some teacher behaviors that can go a long way toward creating a good teaching environment right at the beginning.

1. *Look at the students!* Few things are more disheartening than a speaker who refuses to look at the listeners but instead stares first at a pile of papers, then the ceiling, then an imaginary spot on the floor. Something nice happens when a speaker locks eyes with a listener. Anyone can learn to catch the eye of every student in the room in a matter of seconds.

2. *Don't talk about yourself.* There really isn't much point in telling students that you will be a demanding but fair teacher because they will learn all about you from experience, and not from what you tell them.

3. *Treat students like friends.* A friend can be a critic, but she will never be demeaning or sarcastic. To be critical without hurting feelings is to walk a very fine line. Freshmen easily and often mistake irony for sarcasm and feel hurt when there is no real reason for it.

4. *Work the room.* Students will quickly become disengaged from an instructor who is simply reciting his discipline. They may at first resent being bothered by questions or requests for examples or summaries, but a teacher who engages students and appears to know them as persons will, in the end, be much more effective than one who simply gives notes.

Some teachers might be upset by the persona concept, seeing it as being phony and too much like acting. I simply cannot agree with that position. Lowman (1995) stated the case as directly as anyone: "College classrooms are dramatic arenas first and intellectual arenas second." In its original context it is clear that he does not mean that the teacher should be playacting. But he does mean that the teacher should create a dramatic setting—one where emotions are involved. I suspect that such an environment might even be essential when the thing to be learned involves a cognitive change. Nearly a hundred years ago James (1904) wrote: "In admitting a new body of experience, we instinctively seek to disturb as little as possible our pre-existing stock of ideas." But when new learning *demands* a disturbance of existing ideas, then there must be a cognitive change. Something old must be abandoned. Even in the nineteen-year-old, an old and comfortable way of thinking is not going to be given up easily. A logically compelling handout will not do it. The idea must be presented with panache. The student needs to be moved as well as informed. Eble (1983) made the point as directly as possible, "We spend too much time worrying about the deceit of acting, too little about the impact it enables one human to have on another, too little on how much fun it is, for both actor and audience."

Students, like any audience, see through and resent a presentation that is obviously an act. But any audience can get quite caught up in a virtuoso performance. As Lowman (1995) again noted: "Good lectures are difficult to ignore." What, in fact, could it mean to suggest that someone "work at teaching better" if not the polishing and perfecting of exposition and presentation? The intent is to engage students with course content. If this can best be accomplished by behaving somewhat differently in the classroom, then that enabling behavior would hardly qualify as hypocrisy or phoniness.

Persuasion

A good knowledge of content combined with an engaging exposition will go a long way toward keeping students' minds on the subject. Paying attention is not yet learning, however. An engaging presentation runs the constant risk of becoming entertainment. Few things are more welcome to the freshman than an entertaining teacher. But being entertained is a far cry from being motivated to learn. If the desired synapses are to be stabilized, and so made available for future use, they need to be used repeatedly, in different contexts, and with intervals between. The improved retention that comes when a task is done in segments, with intervals between, is known to psychologists as the *Ziegernak principle*.

It has been noted repeatedly that a great deal of what students learn is learned outside the classroom. Some teachers, however, in the face of student lethargy, have come to believe, as do many of their secondary school counterparts, "if I don't say it, they won't learn it." I'm convinced, however, that there will be no real learning unless students themselves deal verbally with the content, in class and outside, both in speech and in writing. They must become persuaded to do this, and persuading them is the most difficult aspect of teaching.

As suggested earlier, motivation (as here defined) is something that students must initiate. Fortunately, the initiation is not impervious to outside influence. Some teachers manage to do something, or be something, that persuades students to read about, talk about, and write about content, and so learn it. What these teachers have is subtle and difficult to analyze. Even authorities who seem to know about these things tend to be nebulous and metaphorical where the persuasive part of teaching is concerned.

To become motivated to learn, the one thing that a student must experience is a need to learn—feel a desire to know. We are not talking here about studying for an exam. Almost all of them will do some version of that. What we hope for is learning that is effective because it satisfies curiosity. As noted by Klivington (1989), the simple reception of stimuli (hearing something, reading something) is not sufficient for learning, even if repeated. Synapse stabilization seems to require what are called "gating signals" from other parts of the brain—modules involved with focusing attention. In particular, the frontal lobes of the brain must become involved because it is that part of the brain that prevents distraction by random incoming signals that are the result of a constant bombardment of external stimuli. Klivington uses the expression "print now" to suggest circuit stabilization, or learning, and states clearly that it happens only when a number of brain regions become activated. There is, then, a biological basis for the different effects of just reading, and reading with attention. If incoming stimuli are to have a lasting effect—cause circuit stabilization—they must be accompanied by *interest*.

As I noted elsewhere (Leamnson 1995) interest is a peculiar word. We all have interests, but, except for the most primitive, we were not born with them. An interest, whether in geology or baseball, had to be acquired. There is a small chicken and egg problem here. We learn readily that which we are interested in, but we need to have learned about something to be interested in it. How does one get started?

It would appear that our overly ample brain, once again, comes into play. We always try to put absolutely novel experiences into some context. We may not know what something "is," so we search to find something that it is "like." If an absolutely novel experience happens to associate with something we already have an interest in, that prior interest can spill over and prompt us to learn more about the new thing.

To first become interested in ice hockey, for example, an adult would probably need to have some prior interest in other team sports, or maybe just ice skating, or perhaps dance, or maybe a psychological interest in kids at play. With absolutely no aspect of the goings on of ice hockey triggering any previously developed interest, it is probable that the game will come across as little more than pandemonium with weapons.

The trouble with this concept of interest by association, from the point of view of teaching, is that we are dealing with a group of students, and as a group their developed interests, with a couple of notable exceptions, can only be guessed at. There is one element, however, that you can be sure they all have in common—you, the teacher. I noted earlier, and others have made the same point (Eble 1988), that freshmen will start out being more interested in you than in the subject matter. People's natural interest in other people can be a powerful tool for teachers and that fact can be put to good use. Think of the many kids who developed an interest, in baseball or the piano, because a parent clearly exhibited such an interest. Kids don't play sports spontaneously or because they are told to. It was some valued person's interest that was contagious and got things started. One of the surest ways for a student to develop interest is to "catch it" from a beloved teacher.

This idea needs thinking about. It's more subtle than students working hard to please a teacher. That's an old idea (and not to be lightly dismissed) but not quite what's intended here. The student enjoyment underlying the kind of learning I have in mind is indeed in the subject matter itself, and not in the satisfaction that comes from pleasing the teacher. The student in this case is looking to find out what it is that some teacher finds so interesting. This will happen more often if the student finds that the teacher herself is in some way interesting or admirable.

Taking an interest in something because someone else finds it interesting is very frequently observed in budding romances. When a young man is head-over-heels in love, anything his significant other finds interesting will almost immediately become a matter of interest to him. Can there be—should there be—an element of this interest-by-contagion in teaching?

A number of writers (Bloom 1993, Eble 1983, and Schwab 1978) do consider the capturing of the mind of a student to be a kind of intellectual seduction. The very word seduction carries so much emotional freight that one hesitates to even write it. But we simply don't have a good word that denotes what's intended here. If a teacher's persona and passionate love of a subject show through her presentation and her interactions with students, and that makes the subject enticing to students, what do we call that? While completely intellectual, it has elements of seduction—a mind has been won, so to speak. (Both the wonderful and the dangerous elements of this kind of mind-capture are illustrated in two movies: *The Man Without A Face* and *Dead Poets' Society*.)

This idea will come up again. For now it would be well to review how it applies to the goal of educating. Exposition alone, no matter how complete, accurate, or detailed, will be sufficient for only a few students. The rest will be simply transcribing, sometime just semiconsciously, and few will consider the material between classes, or talk about it, or read it on their own. These are the learned behaviors of good upperclassmen—few freshmen start college with habits like these. Doing things differently involves a cognitive change. A *cognitive change* is a particularly difficult kind of learning because it means responding in a new way that uses previously underutilized synapses, and at the same time ignoring stable and well used synapses. Using old and comfortable pathways in a familiar situation would be considerably less stressful than burning in a whole new set of synapses. Cognitive change is a matter of learning the new and ignoring the old. Few people submit gladly to cognitive change so understood.

As noted earlier, students will learn, as declarative knowledge, things they don't really believe. When that happens students have not made a real cognitive change; their procedural knowledge remains untouched (Walvoord and McCarthy 1990). The problem is exemplified when expert exposition alone fails to affect students' study habits. Because study habits are a matter of procedural knowledge, a real cognitive change will be required when students' success in college depends on their studying in a new way.

What's at issue here is getting students to learn in an effective way, a task often referred to as "teaching students to learn." This use of teaching is inconsistent with our definition, for two reasons. Learning is not a content area, and teaching is not something that can be done to someone else. What we teach is literature, or art history, or accounting. How we behave while teaching these disciplines will determine whether students become motivated and so do what it takes to learn. Much of this learning can only be done outside the classroom. It will not get done by reading or writing if these activities are merely mechanical.

Reading and writing will indeed involve some part of the brain because they both involve sensory stimuli. To stabilize synapses, however, sensory perceptions must be accompanied by signals from other parts of the brain that are associated with something slightly more emotional—interest, and so attention. What this means is that reading and writing become learning experiences, in the effective sense, only when there is a certain level of emotional involvement. Ideally, the content itself would be sufficient, but only a few freshmen will have experienced the kick that comes from being intellectually absorbed. I'm sure everyone has the potential for intellectual enjoyment. One might think of it as a pleasure center somewhere in the brain. Whatever it is, it's easily ignored and most freshmen need something like a breakthrough to discover the kind of satisfaction that comes with intellectual activity. An admired teacher with a contagious love of his subject (and a sincere love of students) can be a most effective cause of such a breakthrough.

The teacher persona, it must be added, sometimes educates inadvertently. Freshmen may have poor language skills, and dreadful listening habits, but they are amazingly good at picking up on subliminal signals. It's difficult to hide your true feelings and attitudes from them. According to Margaret McFarlan:

> We don't teach children. We just give them who we are. And they catch that. Attitudes are caught, not taught. If you love something in front of a child, the child will catch that (quoted in McCullough 1995).

And on that elusive goal of critical thinking, Nickerson et al. (1985) suggests: "Remember that attitudes are more effectively projected than taught. Nothing that you say in class is likely to have as lasting an impact on your students' attitudes toward thinking as will those that you consistently display." This talent of students' for "seeing past the words" reinforces the notion that the teacher, while in a sense performing, needs to be quite careful and consistent in developing the teaching persona. Students will lose all respect for someone obviously putting on a phony act.

The last general topic on pedagogy has to do with an old observation authenticated by Richard Light (1990, 1992) and Alexander Astin (1993). Students learn a great deal from one another. *What* they learn, however, is variable. Many modify their political stance during their college years. Some make significant changes in their sets of values, religious convictions, or tastes in music. Many educators have suggested ways to tap into this phenomenon, and get students' mutual learning experiences to go beyond the social and into the academic arena. Most of these techniques can be lumped under the umbrella of *group learning*.

Learning Without Teachers

Properly done, there are few more effective devices for learning than studying in small groups. Anyone who has participated in a small seminar will remember how ideas evolve or become extinct as they go through one brain after another and come out slightly altered. Most memorable of all are those instances when one's own well-constructed idea gets dismantled, amended, pruned, and massaged until it emerges transmogrified, or perhaps moribund. Group study has so much potential for good that it has, in some instances, turned into something of a fetish. I have great faith in group study, but only so long as it remains a means to an end and does not become an end in itself. It's easy to slip into that way of thinking that says, "if a little is good, a lot will be better." Whether it's pedagogy or medicine, this is dangerous thinking. Teachers who believe that study groups or research teams are the answer to their problems are somewhat like certain disciples of John Dewey who took his statement, "students learn what they do, not what we tell them," in a narrow and simplistic way and began to believe that physical activity *in and of itself* was sufficient for learning. Publishers who try to make their textbooks or learning packages completely self sufficient and therefore teacher-proof, provide another example of this kind of tunnel vision. The intent in all these cases seems to be the production of an instrument or process so well-designed that its mere use will guarantee the desired outcome. This is an old idea that was pushed to an absurd level many years ago with the introduction of "teaching machines." These gadgets were premised on the belief that learning was simply a matter of response to sensation. An endlessly patient machine would take a student through a process as many times as necessary to elicit correct responses. Today the rusty remnants of these machines can be found in landfills around the country, and for good reason. There has yet to be found any device that, in and of itself, will cause learning. This is true as well for study groups. Learning is still a matter of self-initiated brain change, and there are no techniques or machines that guarantee that to happen.

Techniques, methods, and materials are effective only to the extent that they induce, or inspire, students to switch on the thinking parts of their brains and process the language of the discipline. It follows that it is not the formation or existence of study groups that determines outcome, but only what each student does in the group environment. The problem then is a common one, in that it involves having students use some method or technique *and* in such a way that they are more apt to focus attention and verbalize concepts. As with all attempts to transmit procedural knowledge, simply *telling* students the advantages of group study does not produce significant results. Young students learn the advantages of group study the way they learn most things, through experience.

To profit from collaborative or cooperative learning, students have to first do it, and secondly they must become convinced that it is worthwhile. Students will indeed learn through experience the efficacy of discussing and debating issues among themselves, but to learn that through experience means first having that experience. What can teachers do to ensure both collaborative work and a successful outcome?

In the case of freshmen, it is nearly essential that the teacher take the initiative. Most students fresh out of high school cannot tolerate anything that smacks of nerdiness. And what could be more nerdy than gathering a few buddies for the express purpose of studying? Freshmen need to be initiated in this regard, and that means a big push from the outside.

Success has been claimed for such a variety of approaches to group study that one has an embarrassment of riches to choose from. What follows is what sounds good to me, and what I have found to be moderately successful.

Group study that fails its purpose, or irritates students, becomes a negative reinforcer. It's important, therefore, that group work be rewarding from the beginning. A few bad experiences are all it takes for a student to associate group study with something unpleasant and to be avoided. Supervising and coaching group work would seem to be the only way to ensure that students get something worthwhile from the practice and so begin to associate it with useful outcomes, which means it would have to be initiated, and practiced, in the classroom with the teacher available.

I am confident enough of the following approach to recommend it. Sort students into groups of three or four with the express purpose of having them prepare for a quiz to be given after a set interval of study, say five minutes. The quiz topic should be loosely delineated in advance so that all the groups will be reviewing the same general content. At the beginning, most will probably appear to be at a loss as to what to do. To prod them along in the right direction I move from group to group listening to what's going on. In many cases, the students' first tendency is to thwart the whole intent by studying privately and quietly even as they sit in groups. So the first step in coaching is to get them talking. I go from group to group suggesting topics or posing sample questions that might appear on the quiz. If the room is not quite noisy within a minute or so, I raise my energy level a notch and start a second round. Once they are talking, more coaching is required to see that they are examining topics in a useful way and not playing "trivial pursuits."

The quiz itself is critical in this process. If it's a giveaway that they could have breezed through with no study at all, they will be further reinforced to believe that this is all just another game teachers play and they can certainly get along without it. If, on the other hand, the quiz is unnecessarily difficult, or addresses the most obscure aspect of the topic, students will again believe that they have simply wasted time. Part of my coaching involves gently nudging them toward the content matter they will be quizzed on. Ideally, the questions members of a study group ask one another will be about how something operates, or why one thing is more important than another, or of the "what would happen if . . ." variety. But it takes a lot of pump-priming to get them to that stage. It's a good idea after the quiz to ask whether they found the study session to be helpful. If not, find out why not. If it did help, that's a good time to remind them that what works in class will work just as well outside of class.

Group work during class time aims primarily at associating good outcomes with certain student behaviors. It certainly should not be a substitute for learning between class periods. In the best of worlds, students would be weaned eventually from teacher coaching and use this kind of cooperative learning simply because it worked. One way to encourage cooperative learning outside class time is to assign a challenging expository paper and urge them to do the research and the thinking part in their study groups. The idea here is that they *study* the problem cooperatively until there is some consensus on the points to be made and the arguments to be developed. Some teachers allow, or even specify, that a single report or essay be submitted for the group as a whole. That approach is fraught with difficulties however. Beyond the endless squabbles over who contributed how much is the simple fact that a group paper defeats the purpose of group study, which is learning by *all* the members of the group. As will be emphasized in detail later, writing is a most effective way to learn. Group reports usually mean that the students who are in most need of practice in verbalizing and articulating ideas will be the least likely to get that important experience. Group discussion and study followed by individual reports would seem to provide optimal results.

A review of the suggestions presented in this chapter will show that these proposals all involve, in one way or another, the struggle with language. It is because I find language development and use to be an essential element in learning that I have devoted so much space to a relatively few pedagogical devices that force the struggle. It might be useful to summarize what I consider the essential elements of good pedagogy.

Summary

1. Frequent ten-minute periods spent in literate, coached dialogue with three or four students can have powerful effects. More students begin to spend some time between classes on course content and all, eventually, get valuable practice at verbalizing otherwise vague and fuzzy ideas.

2. When technical terms are needed, bring them in *after* the relevant concept has been discussed (the "idea first, word last" approach). It encourages good storytelling on the part of the teacher and good listening habits on the part of students.

3. The brain work should be shifted onto the students. They will learn more if they do their own outlining, note-making, and paraphrasing.

4. The teaching persona should be inspiring and persuasive. Even though student motivation is internally initiated it can be powerfully influenced by a teacher's obvious passion for a discipline.

5. Cooperative learning (small study groups and the like) is effective to the extent that it forces verbalization of ideas and holds individual students responsible for their own learning.

If it is beginning to appear that teaching first-year students is hard work, then I have succeeded in making an important point. Barzun (1991) and Elmore (1996) both stress their conviction that teaching and learning are not going to be made easy through innovative approaches and novel methods. Nearly everything imaginable has been tried at least once. And what works best generally turns out to be something that requires considerable effort on the part of students and teachers alike.

It is for this reason that I have been both selective and eclectic in my choice of topics to be included under pedagogy. Even where I have made strong suggestions, these should not be taken as rigorously prescriptive. Prescriptions, as in the medical sense, suggest a self-effecting nostrum, the use of which requires no effort on the part of the user. It is just that way of thinking about learning that cannot succeed. When it comes to freshmen, neither learning nor teaching can be made effortless.

6

THE CLASSROOM

And no matter how enlightened the pedagogy, there is nothing natural about a classroom.

—Alan Cromer

Everything said heretofore, about the brain, language, students, and pedagogy, comes to bear when we consider that dramatic arena, the classroom. Here the students meet you, the great unknown, and you meet a collection of mostly young people with wildly varying genetic endowments and environmental experiences. Much depends on how they react to your teaching. In reflecting on the classroom, many previously made points on learning and pedagogy will have to be reprised, but the emphasis will be on students and their point of view.

In the best situations, most learning goes on outside the classroom. Consider the case where the opposite is true—most of what is learned is learned in the classroom. For that to happen the principal activity in that classroom would have to be the transfer of information. Most freshmen are fairly comfortable with this kind of teaching. It's what they know. They are experienced and competent at picking key words out of the flow, and they will assiduously copy into their notes anything the teacher writes on the chalkboard. As noted earlier, instructors who teach this way will sometimes decide that everything will go faster if lecture notes are simply passed out in advance. The classroom in such cases becomes a tutored study hall. Little or no learning needs to be done between classes, and study continues to mean what it always has, getting ready for the exam a day or two in advance.

By now it is probably not necessary to state that this is not the kind of teaching I would recommend. What such teaching requires of the student is retention and recall, and not the kind of brain workout demanded by real learning. Russell (1991) noted that, at one time, St. John's College of Santa Fe, following the University of Chicago's lead, demanded of every student an essay that "bears traces of this struggle." The classroom environment that I will hold up for emulation will be one where the teacher inspires students to struggle with the discipline, both within and outside the classroom.

Getting Started

Regardless of their reasons for taking your course, the real focus of your students' initial curiosity will be you. "What's he/she going to be like?" is a natural question. Many teachers take advantage of this initial curiosity to do something I will call *metateaching*. I derive this term from "metadiscourse," a practice that writing instructors and editors warn of. When I say, "in these pages . . . ," or "as noted in a previous chapter . . . ," I am engaging in metadiscourse— talking about the fact that I am talking about something. A little goes a long way. In metateaching the content of what one is teaching is the teaching itself. It takes the form of talking about "this class," the instructor's expectations, perhaps a preview of the semester, sometimes a somber warning about how much work the course will require, and maybe an autobiographical sketch.

I believe a teacher misses a chance to make a good start when he treats the first day's period as a kind of throw-away class. Some teachers do not even have anything prepared for the first day and more or less wing it, using this metateaching as a way to use up the time. Nor does having students introduce themselves on the first day achieve very much. It makes them so self-conscious that they never hear what anyone else says. There are better ways to achieve a group identity, the best being getting them to talk to one another as mutual learners. We might speculate here on the effect the above examples of metateaching have on students.

First-year students are not good listeners, particularly in the classroom. The speech of the typical college professor is often too literate for many— too many modifiers and subordinate clauses. They are, however, quite adept at picking up nonverbal signals. I once had students present brief reviews of various topics to the class while I sat off to one side making notes on the presentations. One young man was giving an adequate if somewhat dry presentation, but was repeatedly interrupted by shorts bursts of muffled giggling. Nothing he said was in any way humorous and his demeanor was unremarkable. Still, the giggling continued. Suddenly I saw what was happening. This charming imp was *doing my act*! A pause with a head tilt got a laugh. A hand gesture—another laugh. I was seeing myself in action.

The significant point here is not one student being a good mimic, but the whole class recognizing me in his mimicry. And so it is that students will come to learn about your class and about you. The predominantly oral culture of the young does not prepare them for the more literate discourse of the college classroom and the focused listening such discourse demands. That same culture does demand some expertise, however, in picking up on subliminal cues and reading between the lines. So what kinds of signals are being picked up when the instructor indulges in metateaching?

I don't think they are the signals we should be sending. We certainly don't come across as being eager to get started. Students can infer that we find our teaching, or even ourselves, more important, or interesting, than we find students or the course content.

Contrast metateaching with getting down to business. Imagine a teacher who starts off questioning students, not with the intent of testing them, but to learn something of their background or their level of preparedness. Or one who immediately instructs the class to note some page in the text where there is a map, or a chart, or a photograph, or a poem. Any such activity on day one tends to throw students off the scent, so to speak. Instead of a relaxed period spent psyching out the teacher, or wool gathering, they are suddenly into content—responding, reciting, and reflecting.

Not many first-year students are prepared to "hit the ground running." But if your intent is to engage students both mentally and verbally with the subject you teach, no harm is done in getting down to it on the first day. It may in fact set the right tone and mood for the course. Sitting passively in perfect comfort is not a student habit we should be reinforcing.

Preparing

One of my colleagues, when asked if he prepared his lectures, responded, "I spent nine years in college preparing." This was not an entirely flippant or irrelevant reply. Most of us teach our specialty, or something close to it, and so we are, so far as content and information are concerned, prepared to present it. But while presenting is a form of teaching, we are looking here for optimally effective teaching. As suggested earlier, effective teaching combines content presentation with certain teacher behaviors that inspire or incite students to learn, either at the moment or later, on their own or in groups. Preparation, ideally, would mean planning, at least tentatively, not just the content but methods of presentation that will engage students and cause them to pursue the subject outside of class time. That aspect of preparation is a component of pedagogy, and even college instructors, especially those teaching first-year students, should be thinking about pedagogy.

College instructors vary in their effectiveness and the more effective will in fact be using good pedagogy even if they do so inadvertently, or have arrived at it by a common sense or trial-and-error route. Preparing for class should be one aspect of that pedagogy. Preparing, however, is not intended to suggest that bane of school teachers—the lesson plan. A good preparation need take no more than ten or fifteen minutes, provided the content is well in hand. The purpose of the preparation is to answer a few simple questions. How will I conduct the review? How am I going to tell the new story? What questions should I begin with? What examples or illustrations should I use? At what point do I ask for a review? Does this material lend itself to a brief in-class writing assignment? What are the take home lessons that should stand out? What should the students do on their own to get ready for the next period?

Planning takes a little longer when you're just starting out, but it continues to pay dividends to the veteran, who might be able to do it in ten minutes or so. In any case, the mini-preparation should be done on paper and be available for reference. Sometimes two or three Post-it®s stuck onto content notes or the text are sufficient reminders.

The Optimally Comfortable Classroom

How do the students perceive a teacher so prepared? There's no question that a fair number of them are discomfited by the instructor who comes in with the intent of shaking them up and a plan for getting it done. Review questions directed at specific students hit like a bucket of cold water the first few times. Healy (1990) wrote of developing children: "Good language, like the synapses that make it possible, is gained only from interactive engagement; children need to talk as well as to hear." All of which is equally true of college freshmen. The cold water analogy prompts the question, what is the optimal comfort level for students in a classroom?

Like Goldilocks' bed, it has to be just right. From the point of view of most freshmen, however, it can't get too comfortable. Their preference is to be entertained, or at least not be bothered. Lowman (1995) wrote: "A good lecture is hard to ignore." But that presumes an audience of good listeners, and most freshmen have not yet developed the listening talent. The unpleasant conclusion is that a lecture, good or otherwise, will be perceived by many as just more teacher talk, and so something to be tuned out until the speaker gets down to giving notes. Since notes can be taken in a semiconscious state, many students can sit through a class period and never once engage their minds with the content.

It can be intuited from some basic principles of physics, biology, and psychology that allowing students to sit comfortably and passively is not a good idea. A basic law of physics says that a system will not change unless there is an imbalance of forces, and biology posits a change in students' brains if learning is to occur. *Something* must push or pull them into trying out new circuits, because it's more comfortable to not do it. A classroom where students are learning will have a feel of healthy tension about it. Healthy tension is not debilitating. I have in mind the mental/emotional disequilibrium that pushes us to action or at least prepares us for action, particularly a responsive action that couldn't be completely anticipated. It's a small taste of what I imagine a hockey goalie feels in a breakaway, when a forward is bearing down on him, one-on-one. A student can be kept in a similar, if less anxious, state of readiness if he knows he might be called on anytime, without warning.

This kind of anticipatory tension is something more than alertness. Because much of college learning involves cognitive change—denying or modifying an old belief to accommodate a new one—it is rarely done in a state of utter comfort. I suspect a more dynamic classroom was what Lowman had in mind when he referred to the classroom as a dramatic arena (1995). Some emotional involvement can provide that "gating signal" that Klivington spoke of—a second synaptic signal that helps stabilize an underused synapse (1989). The power of emotional involvement to stabilize circuitry is exemplified by a well-known phenomenon. People remember in remarkable detail where they were and what they were doing when they first heard particularly distressing news, such as the assassination of a prominent figure.

Nothing so traumatic is intended here. Students cannot be kept on the edge of their seats for fifty minutes, but a well-told story combined with frequent interactive discourse, and perhaps interrupted for an in-class short essay or study session, goes a long way toward keeping a group engaged.

The Classroom Mood

My colleagues and I have often wondered at the sometimes remarkable differences in atmosphere between two sections of the same course taught by the same instructor. Some of the differences can be attributed to the time of the day, or swings in the instructor's mood, and the like. But when a difference between classes is observed consistently, it is probably because the student groups themselves are setting the mood. Groups will be different because students are different and the way they sort themselves into classes is mostly a matter of chance. Differences between individual students will be considered later. For now the question is, to what extent can the teacher set or regulate the mood of a classroom and how can it be done if the group itself tends to set its own mood?

As suggested earlier, the way the teacher starts out has a particularly strong effect on classroom mood. You the teacher, at the beginning, are the most interesting thing in the room. It makes sense to capitalize on the curiosity, but not necessarily to indulge it. The peculiar thing about curiosity is that it disappears as soon as it is satisfied. It is for that reason that I have reservations about talking about oneself or doing too much metateaching. Nothing is lost by prolonging curiosity about yourself and your methods. Students will eventually learn what kind of persona you present and how the course is going to develop.

Strange as it might sound, students create the tone in a classroom, but the teacher has the power to determine what they create. First-year students come more or less convinced that a teacher is something of an obstacle. We stand between them and their desires for good grades, credit, and a diploma. They come prepared to see us as adversaries. Without some work on our part the classroom mood can become one of tension and distrust.

There is a practice in some departments that neatly lifts the teacher out of the adversarial role. These are the situations where the giving of tests is taken out of the hands of the teacher. Departmental exams or standardized achievement tests have the desirable effect of deflecting student resentment or distrust that would otherwise fall on the teacher. In my own undergraduate days the physics department held departmental exams outside scheduled class times and in various large halls around the campus. They were distributed by people who were not our teachers and graded by persons unknown. Most of us came to see our individual teachers, not as opponents, but as the "good guys" who were helping us get through all this. I still harbor a fondness for my physics teachers.

Ally or Adversary

Tiberius and Billson (1991) have described the polar extremes of the classroom mood as being an adversarial relationship at one end and something like an alliance at the other. Most teachers would prefer to see themselves as allied with students in the struggle against shallowness and ignorance, and not as an adversary. How can we move toward alliance?

There is no easy path here. Trying to talk students out of their mind-set will work for only a very few. Nothing works quite so well as having performance standards externally derived, but you can get some mileage out of pretending that evaluation is someone else's doing, even when in fact it is not. You can distance yourself a little from the bad guy perception by avoiding the pronouns *I* and *me* in association with evaluation. Expressions such as, "I will give an exam next week" or "I will be grading your papers this weekend," only reinforce in students' minds the idea that you and they are on opposite sides in a contest. The more a teacher can associate herself with course content and the less with evaluation, the more likely it becomes that students will see her as being on their side. Putting exam dates on the syllabus and then pretending that the exam is something that is simply going to happen has merit. Little offhand remarks such as, "*We* have to get ready for this exam coming up" go at least a little way toward convincing students that you, personally, are not the enemy. Alerting students to exams and due dates as if these were "acts of God" might move both the class and the teacher toward the view that they are on the same side.

Learning Styles

That students differ enormously is a fact that we all agree on but seem not to know what to do with. Cromer (1997), in his usual no-nonsense manner, makes his understanding of the problem crystal clear: "Nothing is more evident than that some people are smarter than others, and nothing is more vigorously denied." (By using the man-in-the-street term *smarter* he was appealing to our commonsense and exhibiting a staunch disdain for word mincing.) Whether smart people have something peculiar in the organization of their brains or have simply learned more than others will be debated endlessly. Teachers, however, have no choice but to believe that people can get smart by learning. Students in Europe, and particularly Asia, tend to believe the same. In the United States, however, smartness is widely believed to be something one simply has, or has to some degree. Many students come to college thinking that what they can learn has been delimited in advance by their level of smartness—something fixed and immutable. As Wilson and Daviss suggested (1994), "Academic success is (to students) a matter of inborn ability rather than diligent effort. . . . Either you get it or you don't." One of the primary challenges to getting students to improve their minds is convincing them that such improvement is possible.

The question here is whether or not all people learn the same way. The firm belief that they do not has generated a great deal of research into the question of learning styles (see Schroeder 1993, Dunn and Dunn 1978, Dunn and Griggs 1988). The belief that people learn in different ways—have different learning styles—has produced something of a cottage industry to determine how many such styles there might be. Robert J. Sternberg (1997) has also proposed and described a variety of "thinking styles." How many there are depends on who you talk to. Cromer summed up a discussion on the subject this way: "The categories are clearly conventional, being an invention of the investigator, not nature" (1997). Many years earlier James (1904) made a similar comment on a similar subject: "There is no reason, if we are classing the different types of apperception, why we should stop at sixteen rather than sixteen hundred." The situation gets horrendously complex when combinations of learning styles are attributed to the same individual.

So, do learning styles represent anything real, and if so, do they have any bearing on the way we teach? One thing would appear obvious to anyone who has had to learn or think about topics from various fields of interest.

We certainly use different modes of study—learning styles if you will—when approaching different kinds of material. Learning poetry demands different mental processes than does learning calculus. This fairly obvious idea became a hot topic of research in the 1970s and 1980s with results that, I would suggest, only clouded the issue further. Instead of pursuing the problem of what styles of thinking and learning are most useful for different kinds of content, most research centered on testing and categorizing student *preferences* for ways to learn. As both James (1904) and Cromer (1997) noted, these categories do not represent any brute reality that can be detected, but rather the richness of the investigator's imagination. Cromer noted that Dunn and Dunn (1978) arrived at twenty-three as the number of distinct categories, each with dichotomous preference options. Because a student would express one or the other preference in all the categories, there would be 2^{23} (over eight million) possible learning style preference states. What does anyone do with this kind of information?

The error in most discussions of learning styles is, I'm convinced, one of misplaced mapping. In the literature on this topic, learning style is generally considered not only a property that maps onto a student, but one that is innate, or even physiological. Dunn and Griggs (1988) claimed, for example, "Learning style is a *biologically and developmentally imposed* set of characteristics that make the same teaching method wonderful for some and terrible for others (emphasis added)." My earlier comments should have made it clear that I believe learning styles map properly onto topics or subjects and not onto people. Even those researchers who put great stock in learning styles will add a caveat, usually in an aside near the end. They often note that, ideally, a student would develop different learning styles and not rely on their preferred method to carry them through any potential challenge. As Katz and Henry (1988) put it: "A group of students who have not had very productive college experiences . . . are those who have few traces of a complex thinking style. They may use only one thinking mode unchecked by or unintegrated with any other thinking mode." Precisely so. I find this a reasonably explicit admission that learning styles vary with content to be learned, and that people are not, in fact, saddled at some early age with an unmodifiable learning style.

The significance of this research for the college classroom instructor is perhaps obvious; a learning style preference might simply be a proxy for sub-

ject preference. The argument that an interest develops as a result of a biologically determined learning style is no more convincing than its opposite,
that learning styles develop as a result of interests that required those styles.
Most of us like doing what we do well and can be put out of sorts when asked
to do the unfamiliar.

But doing the unfamiliar is what learning is. A liberal education, one
that liberates through empowerment, cannot consist in accommodating only
those interests a student brings to the enterprise. My position is that learning styles are themselves learned. And if you can learn one, you can learn
two, or seven.

What then is the classroom instructor to make of the notion of learning
styles? That one's content matter can be taught in ways that would accommodate all the possible learning styles seems preposterous on the face of it.
Colorful sobriquets notwithstanding ("Rocks for Jocks," "Physics for Poets"),
geology cannot be taught *as if* it were physical education, and physics cannot be taught *as if* it were literature. The only rational approach is to bite the
bullet and conclude that teaching our subject, particularly to first-year students, means teaching how the subject is learned as well as what is to be
learned. If one good thing comes out of the learning style debate it might be
that more teachers realize that many students are struggling as much with
how a subject is learned as with what is to be learned.

It is altogether understandable that few us reflect deeply on how our
subject gets learned. We've probably had an abiding interest in it for many
years and what we do seems so natural as to be unremarkable. But questions like, "how does a philosopher learn philosophy?" or "how does a
chemist learn chemistry?" are not trivial. A great deal might be gained if
teachers developed a reasonably precise formulation of the mental and physical activity involved in their own learning. Sharing our own learning
processes with students could prove beneficial. Should students come to
understand that all subjects have their own learning modes, the benefits
might be enduring.

As noted earlier, however, it's not enough to tell students how a subject
is learned. The most carefully reasoned exposition of a learning method is
still teacher-talk to many. They learn little more from it than they would learn
about playing the cello by watching Yo Yo Ma do it. The most difficult challenge for teachers is designing activities that cannot be done without using
the mental process one wishes to have developed.

One more thing before leaving the topic of learning styles. The same content is often better understood, and understood by more students, if it is repeated using different approaches each time. This advice was also given a hundred years ago by William James when he wrote: "The only really useful practical lesson that emerges from this analytic psychology in the conduct of large schools is the lesson already reached in a purely empirical way, that the teacher ought always to impress the class through as many sensible channels as he can" (1904).

Getting to Know Them

A teacher cannot know, in a useful way, who might have an aversion for a course, or for the teacher's persona, unless he first knows the students as people. And knowing means naming.

Getting to know the names of new students, particularly in large sections, is a daunting task. You need a technique—a learning style—no matter what the numbers. One colleague takes photographs of every class at the beginning of the semester. With a photo that has names on the back, learning names is just a matter of frequent practice, the same technique we would use to learn historical characters or the cranial nerves. The more common practice is to use a seating chart. I usually give students a week to sort themselves out and then ask that they stop moving about and take a "permanent" seat. During a class period they print their own names in the appropriate boxes on a chart. Passing out copies of the seating chart helps with the socialization of the group. Classrooms seem less artificial to me when students can refer to something that Terry or Jennifer said, rather than to what "he" or "she" said.

The seating chart does not always work to perfection. Those who attend only periodically show up in someone else's place, and movable chairs can turn the first few minutes of a session into something out of a Marx Brothers movie. But the fact that I keep trying every semester suggests that some good comes from having a seating chart. Getting into the room a few minutes early allows me to spend some time trying to fit names to faces and positions in the room.

How and when to use students' names is another matter of some delicacy. Students can be of two minds about your knowing who they are. It eliminates half of the quiet anonymity they generally find comforting, but it also draws them closer to the teacher, which a lot of them secretly long for. Many freshmen, particularly those living away from home, need a grownup in their lives—someone who seems to have concern for them and cares about what happens to them. For a few, the need might be pressing. Now and then one will latch on to you like a lost puppy for no other reason than that you knew his name and congratulated him on a good response.

Nothing makes much sense but for teachers to believe that what they do—their teaching—will positively affect students' learning. But to know that we are having an effect requires an appreciation of ourselves as others perceive us. And, as Robert Burns wrote in the poem "To a Louse":

> Oh wad some power the giftie gie us
> to see oursels as ithers see us.

How then might students perceive the teacher who knows their names? While thinking about that effect, I was reminded of the bartender in my favorite graduate school hangout. He took lunch orders at the bar and asked for a first name and initial, which he wrote on the order. When the order came up the name was read over the public address system and the patron picked up the order. This gave the bartender two opportunities to associate a name with a face. After a few visits patrons found themselves being greeted by name as soon as they came in. The effect was wonderful. And so it is that Matthew, feeling down and isolated, will get a bit of lift if you can say, "Good morning, Matt" when he comes in. He may consider you someone worth listening to. You in turn might begin to think him worthy of your best effort. A face seems to become a person when it has a name.

From the point of view of the group, however, this kind of treatment can be seen as favoritism if it is not spread around evenly. There is no substitute for alertness and diligence on this point. Nothing splits a group more decidedly than a teacher who appears to favor some students over others in the classroom. Make a special effort to get to know the quiet, unsmiling ones.

Teaching Styles

As surely as students have individual preferences as to content and what they like to study, or at least find easier to study, so teachers will have a preferred way of presenting course content. And if learning styles map onto content, the same would seem obvious for teaching styles. Anything suggested in the way of pedagogy and classroom methods needs to be considered in light of the subject being taught.

Teaching style is used here as something of a catch-all to comprise whatever it is that the teacher is doing. It has come down as folk wisdom that the fixed tradition in college, no matter the content, is something called "the lecture." Few things have muddied the educational waters so much as the notion that the lecture is a given thing—a constant—that is completely knowable by its name. But a great deal of presumptuous and erroneous talk about lectures springs from an inescapable truth—there is a lot of bad lecturing going on in colleges.

The contemporary reaction to bad lectures has been analogous to that of William H. Kilpatrick (see Russell 1991) to the schooling of Dewey's day after Dewey criticized it. Instead of studying and critiquing instruction with a view toward improving it, Kilpatrick saw instruction as intrinsically flawed and so in need of replacement and not repair.

Similarly, the college lecture has fallen on hard times with few defenders willing to let their voices be heard. Any number of replacements have been suggested for "the sage on the stage," as college teachers have been characterized. Those who keep an eye on the literature of the field will be familiar with the many alternatives proposed. These have all been described in detail in numerous books and articles, but a useful exercise might be to find commonalties in these approaches: do they all, for example, address the same problem? I have come to believe that they do, and the problem they address is again language facility and use. My position is that this problem be addressed as directly as possible. Not all agree.

Paradigms

The growing interest in increasing the efficacy of college teaching has led Barr and Tagg (1995), and others, to propose that the whole process be rethought. They advocate, somewhat grandly, a paradigm shift. They suggest that a teacher's methods will place her predominantly in either the teaching paradigm or the learning paradigm. It would be wise, again, to keep in mind that the very existence of two paradigms might be the invention of whoever saw the problem in those terms, and not some real thing you could point to. But, real or not, the proposed distinction focuses a question that is decidedly real. Few college teachers start their careers substantially versed in the biological and psychological subtleties of cognitive processes, particularly as these relate to the naïve learner. Most of us have conveniently forgotten our own early struggles with learning. Only with effort can we recreate the mental state of the first-year student. Having for the most part forgotten what it's like to be a freshman, we tend to concentrate on what needs to be presented, or covered, to use the common term, and not so much on how to present it in a way that elicits learning. A few college teachers even defend an apparent indifference to pedagogy by claiming that they can only present and explain and the rest is up to the students. It may well be true, for advanced, literate, and highly-motivated students, that presentation and explanation will suffice. I suspect, however, that the cry for a new paradigm springs from the growing realization that students are now coming to college less prepared for the typical college professor than ever before. Many drop out, I believe, because too much is left up to them at the outset.

I would prefer to recast the argument in terms of the definitions proposed earlier. Teachers should see education as a two person problem, but one where those who are to be educated are much less prepared to follow than the teachers are to lead. This statement of the problem is less dramatic than the paradigm model, but for that reason it points more directly, and unencumbered with metaphor, toward things that individual teachers can do to get first-year students hooked on learning.

The paradigm shift endorsed by Barr and Tagg (1995) implies an increased emphasis on learning—certainly a good thing—but it subtly suggests a deemphasis on teaching. Any scheme that suggests, even accidentally or inadvertently, that college instructors deemphasize teaching is bound to cause confusion and mischief.

I have, of course, overstated the case. The real target of the criticism that leads to suggestions of massive overhauling, is one particular kind of teaching, what has come to be called the traditional lecture. But even this limited criticism paints with too broad a brush. As Lowman (1995) pointed out, and as anyone who has attended one knows, "A good lecture can be magnificent." It is, as he also noted, "difficult to ignore." Mark Ptashne can keep a thousand people in rapt attention while he discourses on the intricacies of viral infection of bacteria. But, if a good lecture can be magnificent, a bad one can be deadly.

If the problems with lecturing are not intrinsic to the thing itself, what then are the problems? Here are five things that can go wrong:

1. Written lectures read from the page.

2. Lectures cast at an inappropriate level.

3. Lectures that are not interactive.

4. Lectures that are boring.

5. Lectures that constitute the sole method of delivery.

I. LECTURES READ FROM THE PAGE

It's hard to imagine that anyone would read a prepared lecture to first-year students. Almost anything else is better.

2. INAPPROPRIATE LEVEL

No matter how the content is delivered, and even if you believe that the optimal method in a particular case is talking, consider the mental state of the audience. Students lack your background and vocabulary, and possibly your interest in the subject. Don't think about what you know, or what's vitally important. Think about what they don't know—about, precisely, what they need to hear. It takes a virtuoso performance to keep first-year students focused during even a portion of a full period.

3. NONINTERACTIVE LECTURES

Even a virtuoso performance can be made a better learning experience if it becomes interactive. Vibrant lecturers move around, work the room, talk to individuals and do their best to get them to talk back, pass out a handout, or break for a practice quiz as a way to review. The difference between the teacher talking 99 percent of the time versus only 85 percent of the time can be remarkable.

4. BORING LECTURES

It would be helpful to know the secret to not being boring, but even without that secret, a boring speaker can be described, by way of negative examples. The first utterance is often a clue. If it is a loud, prolonged, "UUHHH," one's spirits start to droop immediately. Verbal tics like uh, umm, andah, okay?, and phrases repeated purely out of habit, "in other words," "as a matter of fact," and the like, are terribly distracting. They pull the mind away from the content, and a lecture that does not deliver its content will certainly come across as boring.

A boring speaker appears to be unaware of the audience. I have gone voluntarily and at some cost to a lecture because of a keen interest in the topic, only to fall asleep (literally) because the speaker seemed to be talking to himself. This kind of speaker either has no real personal enthusiasm for the subject or has some chronic problem with letting his enthusiasm show. Sometimes he is unconsciously self-conscious, that is, noticeably more concerned with the fact that he is speaking than with enlightening an audience.

If I belabor the point, it is only because students, particularly first-year students, so often use the word "boring" as a generic damning epithet for a course they disliked. For sure, they might mean by it only that they were not continually entertained, but their inability to accurately articulate a problem does not mean that there is no problem. No teacher should be in the business of entertaining, but neither can any be forgiven being boring.

It's risky to suggest positive examples because the attempt to mimic someone else's style might come across as phoniness, but one never-boring speaker comes quickly to mind. Garrison Keillor, of "Prairie Home Companion" fame, never tells a joke, and his stories seem to be train-of-thought ramblings, but he connects with the listener so intimately that you believe that you're *the one* he is talking to. How could you not listen? The virtuoso speaker gets into your head and plays on your neurons like a skillful harpist.

5. LECTURES AS THE ONLY MODE OF DELIVERY

Even a good format wears thin with unvarying repetition. First-year students, furthermore, are not skillful listeners. The well-turned phrase can be like the bloom that wastes its fragrance on the desert air. Because few of them enter the classroom expecting to be captivated, students bring their personal concerns with them and slip easily into private reveries. Frequent eye contact will reveal the "glazed" look we all get to know, and that's a good indicator that it's time to do something different.

Doing Something Different

The most efficient way to learn is to talk with someone who knows what you don't. According to Brookfield (1990): "It is helpful to think of a good educational experience as being like a good conversation." For this reason I am convinced that teachers talking to students will remain an essential aspect of classroom teaching. So my suggestions for varying teaching style are only intended to get students to do something *in addition to* listening, not *other than* listening. Real listening in no way implies passivity.

These are not cutting edge ideas—certainly they imply no new paradigm. I simply suggest a teaching style that capitalizes on the keen insights of perceptive people, gained over a long period of time.

1.   Changing students' brains is the goal.

2.   Understanding and use of language are essential for critical listening, reading, and stabilizing concepts through spoken and written articulation.

3.   Repetition, particularly using different modes of delivery, aids the memory.

4.   The thoughts that are important are those that go on in the heads of students.

These are the truths we should live by. Teaching that consistently ignores any of these elements will be less than optimal.

The Baby and the Bath Water

Ortega y Gasset (1987) urged would-be problem solvers to concentrate their efforts on what he called "nodal problems." A *nodal problem* is a key one that spawns a number of other problems that may be less critical, but are more noticeable in their consequences. He suggested that we think like physicians and treat the disease, not the symptoms. It's excellent advice, but it assumes a talent for distinguishing a nodal problem from its consequent or peripheral offspring.

In an assembly plant, for example, the nodal problem in a low productivity situation is always the slowest step. Putting the entire plant on overtime is a terribly wasteful solution if the desired output could be attained by adding just two workers at the slowest step. Great mischief can be done when a hasty diagnosis mistakes the basic concept behind an enterprise for a nodal problem somewhere within it. It takes a keen insight to see that a system is foundering, not because it is fundamentally flawed, but because it has a few nodal problems.

By hindsight we might conclude that Kilpatrick made this kind of mistake when he set out to *replace* traditional classroom instruction instead of fixing its nodal problems. And what goes around, comes around. The typical contemporary college classroom might be a less-than-ideal learning environment for today's students, but the idea that it represents a nodal problem, that it is intrinsically flawed and needs a complete overhaul, comes across as extreme. Creating a vacuum where there was once a classroom presents an irresistible temptation for anyone with a theory, or infatuated with the latest fad.

Most techniques that become fads started out as effective pedagogical methods but got hyped into something like obsessions. The highly effective practice of learning outside of class time in small study groups has, for example, been used by students of engineering, science, and mathematics for a long time. Alexander Astin (1993) in his massive statistical study of what works for college students, found that one of the most common traits among successful students was their practice of learning in small groups outside of class. Richard Light (1990–1992) found the same thing in his study of Harvard students and graduates. I agree completely with the proponents of cooperative or collaborative learning and support any attempt to encourage all students to profit from the practice. I would further agree that few freshmen stumble onto the practice on their own, or do it intuitively. Classroom practice in small group study is certainly in order. But neither cooperative learning nor any other single practice constitutes the Rosetta stone of education. When a method, useful as it might be, expands to fill all the available time, it begins to look like an obsession. One college instructor claims (undocumented) that *at least* 97 percent of his classroom time is spent in team projects, group work and other forms of collaborative study.

Some innovations derive from the perception that the traditional classroom is teacher-centered, when it should be learner-centered. But is this proposed dichotomy real? A few eccentric teachers may see students as no more than an audience for their performance, but that view is hardly the norm. Most of us realize that students come to us for knowledge, explanation, and enlightenment. The classroom does not represent a zero sum game where learner-centeredness can be achieved only by marginalizing the teacher. *Learner-centeredness,* detrivialized, means that it is students who are struggling with the language and giving their brains a workout. If a well-done lecture achieves that end, the classroom does not thereby become teacher-centered in any pejorative sense.

In short, the optimal teaching style cannot be prescribed, because what is optimal depends on conditions that vary. Class size, room arrangement, course content, and the collective personality of the student group all have to be considered when struggling to find the best way to teach in a given situation. Even the physical and emotional limitations of the teacher have to go into the equation. I suspect, even in light of these many caveats, that the most effective teaching will be done by teachers who vary their approach, use different methods of instructing within the same class period, and never let their students get too comfortable.

Assignments

Rarely does a college instructor assign readings, research, and papers to be written simply because it's always been done—tradition. Out-of-class work is assigned because there is some thing to be learned by doing it. But this out-of-class work also has a secondary purpose. It is used to evaluate in some way the effort students put into the work, and the success they achieved. For beginning students, however, it is the evaluative aspect, and that only, that drives their efforts. For a considerable number, their prior experiences have led them to see the assignment as an instrument of gratuitous torment. At best it is like dues—something owed the instructor. Teachers themselves can worsen this unhealthy perception by calling late or missing assignments work that is "owed" them.

Of the two purposes of assignments, students understand the evaluation part clearly, but at first very few appreciate the learning intent. If assigned to write a report on an article, monograph, or book chapter, most will read the assigned material only to be able to write the report, and not to learn the author's views. They frequently ignore altogether reading assignments that have no evaluative element. Teachers of freshman literature are often appalled at the small number of students who have actually read a story assigned only for classroom discussion. For many, exertion without the reward of a grade is simply energy gone to waste.

Teachers of less experienced students should not be content with inviting students to learn and suggesting ways to do it. We really need to almost force them to learn, at least until learning becomes familiar, then natural, then satisfying. But, obviously, we cannot literally force anyone to learn. What can be done was briefly mentioned earlier—assign work that cannot be done without their engaging their brains.

So how might that be done? To see how it is *not* to be done we might recall here some scenes from bad movies set in classrooms. In a common scene, a bell rings to signal the end of the period, and over the din of shuffling, book slamming, and chattering, the teacher shrieks, "and for tomorrow read chapter six and write a two-page summary!" Who could believe that the teacher in this scenario had carefully planned an exercise that required student learning? It is more like what Eric Severeid called in a college commencement address "the final flick of the proctor's lash."

As surely as there are good and bad lectures, there are good and bad assignments. Bad assignments are bad indeed because they fail to capitalize on a valuable learning opportunity while they alienate students who see them as nothing more than instruments by which they will be evaluated, or, worse, as mere busy-work. The least effective assignment, either reading or writing, is the one that has as its only goal that students do *something*. The good assignment has as its goal specific learning that will result from specific student behavior. Such things need planning—they don't just happen. The following suggestions, as always, should be considered in light of the course content, class size and other such variables.

PLAN AHEAD

Even when a good assignment just "comes to you" during a class period, pretend—behave as if—it has been carefully designed and thought out. Students are more likely to take it seriously if they believe you do. Ideally the goals of an assignment and the activities necessary to achieve them will have been worked out in advance. Imagine yourself doing the assignment and think about what you would do to learn well and retain that learning. Including in the assignment a brief description of how *you* would go about doing the assignment helps students in their own learning.

Whenever possible distribute a written description of the assignment. Students generally find the following elements helpful.

I. *The Topic.* Letting students pick the assignment topic can send the wrong message. If the teacher is not concerned with their learning something specific, students are not likely to be either. When told to write on a topic of their own choosing, a few will indeed take the opportunity to learn about something of general importance. Many, however, will see the exercise as busy-work. Assigning a carefully delineated topic, the same for all, suggests that it is the topic itself that is important, and not just the *doing* of an assignment.

2. *The Intent.* Telling students what it is you want them to learn might seem to be emphasizing the obvious. But remember, it's obvious to you because it's familiar. In the minds of students lurks the question, "Why should I do this?" Give them a reason.

3. *The Audience.* The matter of audience will be taken up in detail in chapter 7. For now it is sufficient to say that students will get a clearer picture of your intent if you make explicit some person or persons, real or imaginary, that could profit from reading the students' assignment.

4. *Scope or Extent.* "How long does this have to be?" is the first question freshmen ask about a writing assignment. I don't think it is a good idea to cater to such perceived needs. I'm not just being perverse here. To answer anyone's question implies some level of acceptance of the premises embedded in that question. Student questions about the precise length of an assignment betray their belief that length is its essential element. To answer the question is to agree with that thinking. The writing should be as extensive as it takes to achieve the goals of the assignment, but few students find that a comforting or useful answer. A certain vagueness in matters of length will direct their thinking toward content. "Two or three pages," or "No more than five pages," serves to suggest what it will take to do an acceptable job, and to discourage them from counting words or pages and feeling "done" when they hit the magic number.

5. *Due Date, Final or Draft, Value.* Less experienced students dwell inordinately on the evaluation of their work. And while working for grades is not the best of motives, neither should it be dismissed. Providing an estimate of how much the assigned work will affect their overall grade eliminates at least one of their uncertainties. The due date must be explicit. The advantages of their doing two drafts will be taken up in chapter 7, but it should be made clear whether it is their first or a second draft that will be evaluated (graded).

When a group is given a clear and detailed assignment by way of a printed handout, with sufficient time to discuss the details and ask questions, some of them, at least, might begin to see assignments as serious learning opportunities. It's another case of them "catching" something from a serious teacher. (The appendix contains two sample assignment handouts that illustrate most of the points made here.)

Teaching the Advantages of Cooperation

As I argued in chapter 5, we should encourage students to study in small groups and provide them opportunities to practice. Small-group study is an excellent way to learn, but few new students are quick to discover that for themselves. Some in-class practice at group work, or problem-solving in teams, so long as it does not become an obsession, has a good effect. That effect is seldom immediate, however. Some students become flustered the first time they are put into small groups and told to discuss or study something. Patience. Work the room. See that they are getting to know one another. Drop some leading questions. Group work in class time works best when students actually feel that this is a good way to address a given problem or achieve a known goal. When it becomes the standard, nearly invariant method for dealing with content, they may well come to see it as one more classroom routine, different in kind from the old fashioned lecture, but a routine nonetheless. I would advise against any routine. Different content and different goals require different means.

What to Teach

The academic freedom enjoyed by college and university instructors would seem to put the matter of syllabi and course content off limits. Except in those (increasingly rare) cases where departments have common syllabi and exams, teachers teach what they think is important. When teaching first-year students, the survey course seems to be the default approach. On survey courses I would agree with Weingartner (1992): "I will . . . register here the skeptical view that the history of *everything*, once over lightly, does not teach the history of *anything*, nor what historical processes are." At this writing a number of colleges and universities have for some years been requiring beginning students to take at least one seminar course in their first-year. One of the characteristics of the typical freshman seminar is that it is *not* a survey course. Most often some topic or small set of topics is studied in depth, through interactive discussions, classroom presentations by the students, and focused writing. As Weingartner further notes, there is really nothing external (barring the above-mentioned departmental exams) driving what he calls "the most formidable enemy of competency. . .the drive toward coverage." He further suggests that the "once over lightly" approach is sometimes favored only because it is easier to teach a little about a lot than to go into fewer things in depth.

How might students react to the two approaches—a little about a lot versus a lot about less? I am not familiar with studies on this specific variable, but I have tried both methods and have come to some tentative conclusions. Beginning students consider the in-depth course to be "too hard," according to their course evaluations. They do not, furthermore, except for selective honors groups, take to it readily. They cling to the textbook as to a life raft and are discomfited by the teacher who skips around in the book or brings up material not in the book. Such a teacher is not playing the school game by the rules they know. But if a teacher persists, the students, who themselves persist, acknowledge that they have, in fact, learned a lot (their way of characterizing understanding in depth). "Learning a lot" is still thought by some to be beyond the call, and these students will often characterize the course as being unnecessarily difficult. Because he states the case precisely and elegantly, I will quote Weingartner at some length here. After stating that new college students are generally not ready for learning at the college level, he continues:

> Accordingly, a signal, and not merely a symbolic one, must be given to the newly arrived, to the effect that most of them will encounter a significant break between the ways of the educational phase recently concluded and those of the educational venture now beginning. First-year student seminars are an effective method for meeting this goal and can initiate students into higher education by being a concentrated *example* of it—a focused study of a quite specific topic in a small class, working in seminar, that is participatory in fashion, under the supervision of an experienced faculty member. This course would not be *about* thinking and learning, discussion and writing, but would *consist* of thinking, learning, discussing, and writing, in circumstances in which feedback would be well-nigh continuous. One must not be deluded into the belief that writing proficiency or critical thinking, for example, might be "acquired" in such a seminar for all future purposes. But the value of

insisting, at the outset, on intensive practice of these capacities not only has immediate pedagogic value, but the kind of exemplary power that makes it an appropriate introduction to things to come, to the way of higher education (1992).

Given our academic freedom, a reasonably small class can always be taught as if it were a seminar, even when not officially so designated.

What Students "Catch" from Teachers

Edward Fisher, a longtime professor at the University of Notre Dame, tells of the uneasiness of a young colleague when the new teachers were told by their dean that they would "of necessity be examples to their students." The young professor's misgivings are not difficult to understand. Major league athletes of star status quickly become role models and they are told that youngsters will emulate them, even if that should include public brawling, drug use, and the like. These same celebrities then believe that they can simply step out of the role of model by disclaiming it. But it can't be done. It is a lot of individuals, acting independently or in concert, but without anyone's permission, that creates a role model. Whether a teacher or an athlete is a role model is completely out of the hands of those teachers and athletes. Just as beauty lies in the eyes of the beholder, role models are created by persons outside the role models' control.

Students are very aware of their teachers. The teacher and what he does often occupy their minds as much as the subject being taught. They talk about their teachers among themselves and to other teachers. When all goes well they come to respect their teachers, where respect, you recall, is really love tinged with restraint. Most of them want it to go both ways—humans, student or otherwise, want to be loved. And as Highet (1966) noted, the young are easy to love.

Should such a healthy situation come to pass, students will inevitably see past the course content and to what the teacher believes or holds in high esteem. There is, frightening as the notion might be, a moral aspect to teaching. I doubt that it is possible to teach in an arresting way without letting ones values seep in.

For these reasons what we say in the classroom and how we respond to students should be a matter of considerable attention. Sarcasm, directed at either the whole group or individuals, always hurts someone—all the more when the source has earned the respect of students. Worse yet, it might send the message that such treatment of others is acceptable. If you do it, why shouldn't they?

Students, unfortunately, often see sarcasm, rudeness, or invective where none is intended. Many have come from a background where self-esteem was a high-priority goal and criticism of any kind was systematically avoided. They are not used to being told they are wrong. But there are no disciplines where any one opinion is as good as any other. Simply trying to correct a student's confused thinking can be perceived as a kind of disrespect, so it's important to remember that saving face is important to students. Even when they are dead wrong, it doesn't hurt to let them have the last word, even if that only means letting them respond to a question like, "Do you see what I mean?" The optimal student/teacher relationship in a classroom is one of delicate balance, and not easy to describe. But treating them kindly, if firmly, goes a long way toward earning their respect. Even the "dumb question"—the one you just answered—needs to be treated lightly and without recrimination. We've all asked silly-by-hindsight questions one time or another. A dumb question is better than no question at all.

Student/teacher relationships are pedagogically important. According to Weingartner:

> Much learning is hard work; most people, not to mention adolescents, are more inclined to work "for" someone known and respected than merely in pursuit of a disembodied goal, possibly including a grade. Even within the limited framework of a lecture, if students are to be brought to active learning, it is vital that the relationship between lecturer and student be more personal than it usually is (1992).

This is good advice. Nothing in it suggests coddling the lazy, but neither does it back away from letting students see their teachers as role models. None of my observations or comments are intended to suggest that, as teachers, we actively teach any moral system or try to inculcate our own values. The message is simply: "Watch what you're about; susceptible young minds are taking it all in."

Who's in Charge?

Earlier I suggested that students know what they want but may not know what is good for them. As teachers in college or university classrooms, it is our obligation to determine what students need to know. The classroom, therefore, is not a democracy. The teacher is in charge, and being in charge means first of all being alert to what's going on. Being alert includes listening for sounds other than your own voice. Mumbled conversation might mean that some students are lost or have tuned you out, and are involved in personal or other extraneous concerns. Students do not like it when things get out of hand, teacher and class going separate ways. Like all young people, they appreciate a measure of discipline.

At the same time they also resent the teacher who lays down the law on day one. College classrooms seldom have anything like the discipline problems one sees in the lower grades. The assumption that they will behave as adults will usually be borne out. Still, it's the teacher's job to let it be known, as the occasion demands, that it is in the students' best interest to stay engaged with the classroom activity, whether that's discussing or problem-solving in groups, or listening.

Special Needs

Every teacher will, sooner or later, have in his class one or more individuals who are laboring with a handicap. Disabilities like palsy and blindness cannot be hidden, but students might have poor hearing, bad eyesight, dyslexia, or any number of hard-to-diagnose learning disorders. These less obvious handicaps are easily overlooked by anyone not so burdened. All the more reason for knowing students as individuals, making frequent eye contact, and being generally observant as to what's going on. Hearing problems are particularly difficult to detect because students who do not hear well may not even be aware of their deficiency. This is another good reason for interactive discussion. Someone who cannot hear what everyone else can should be moved forward and consulted frequently to see that he/she is getting the message. Someone who continually squints at projected images or words on the board, or who tilts his eye glasses to read, will profit from a discrete private query about the last time he had an eye exam. Students who speak well, with insight and understanding, but whose writing is incomprehensible, might be dyslexic or near-illiterate with respect to the written word. Some students are fluent in spoken English but write coherently only in their first language. A few students have an almost pathological fear of tests. They freeze up, stare uncomprehendingly at the questions, jot down scraps of fact unrelated to the question, and generally appear to know nothing of the subject.

In a class of fifty students you can expect three to five to have, to a more or less severe degree, a reading problem unrelated to intelligence, opportunity, or effort—known as dyslexia. Dyslexics appear to have a difficulty of unknown etiology that impairs their ability to perceive written words as arrangements of phonemes. Common words are seen as novel and the dyslexic's reading is understandably slow and laborious. One of my most brilliant students, who later earned his doctorate at UCLA, was a moderately-severe dyslexic. He greatly appreciated having questions whispered in his ear during exams, and an opportunity to talk things over outside of class. Be especially accommodating if a student asks you what a certain exam question means.

Certainly no systematic way of teaching can address all the known and potential clinical conditions that might obtain in a classroom. By keeping alert, however, and asking the right leading question (always in private), a teacher can learn things that explain the otherwise inexplicable. Nothing but good is gained by treating these exceptional cases as what they are—exceptional. One student improved his performance substantially when he was allowed to take his exams in the far corner of the room, facing the wall. People around him simply unnerved him during exams. Finally, every teacher should get expert advice on the handling of epileptic seizures. They can happen at any time and the afflicted seldom warn anyone of the possibility.

Quizzes, Exams, and Grades

"Studying for exams" is the only academic activity in any school situation is a belief so widespread among beginning college students that one might be tempted to believe it's a genetic condition. Teachers might consider tests and exams a gauge for measuring progress, but many students see them only as fodder for generating grades, which they then consider a crude estimate of their personal worth. Trying to talk them out of that frame of mind seldom does any good. A widespread attitude about exams was summarized, somewhat cynically, by Page Smith (1984) who suggested that students see finals week as a period of total cranial purging that flushes the head of a semester's accumulated detritus and clears up space for the coming semester. Not many students start out seeing learning as synapse stabilization and therefore as permanent brain change. Most treat their brains like temporary storage bins. Because they cannot be talked out of this habit, the only solution is for the teacher to force the issue and make them learn differently.

How can this be done? If there were an easy way it would have long ago appeared in *Time* and *Newseek* and all the daily newspapers, and it would have been universally adopted. But as Barzun wrote, teaching well and learning well both involve doing difficult things. The purported breakthroughs that make their way into the media are little more than pedagogical snake oil if they promise success through use of a new and easy technique. The reason teaching (and learning) at the college level is difficult is that so much of it means trying to bring about cognitive change. For example, I previously suggested that beginning students consider *all* knowledge to be declarative as opposed to procedural. But *procedural* means useful in any sense, including useful for answering a question or solving a problem. Many students consider knowledge not as something to be *used* to answer a question, but as something that *is* the answer to a question. Subtle as it might be, the distinction exposes a difference that is real and highly significant. I see no way to cure students of a declarative mind-set except to give them tasks that demand procedural thinking.

Switching to a procedural way of knowing involves a cognitive change on the part of students and so it cannot be done instantly or without a small jolt to the system. The gentlest way to change their approach is to give frequent short quizzes that require them to write out answers to questions that cannot be answered by declaring the facts they know, but only by applying those truths to new or hypothetical situations. Questions of this sort are not particularly easy to come up with. Nor do students, at the beginning, see the point. Beginners in college tend to look for a recognizable term and then do what one colleague calls a "mind dump." Whatever facts they have in their heads about a topic go onto paper, regardless of the question actually asked. A question like, "What would Adam Smith have thought about X?" where "X" is some current situation, is not a question typical freshmen are prepared to deal with. They will tell you what they know about Adam Smith, or about "X." But the hypothetical-deductive nature of this kind of question demands procedural knowledge—knowledge about *both* Adam Smith and "X" *and* the use of both bits of information to answer a novel question. To many, this is not the way the game is supposed to be played.

Good quiz questions of this sort are easier to conjure up in some disciplines than in others, but the teacher who is successful at it is likely to generate some grumbling early on. Beginning students complain that these are "trick questions," or that they had not been given the "right answers." And it is often beginning teachers who design these kinds of questions, because they resemble the sorts of things graduate students and postdoctoral students wrestle with.

Unavoidable in any consideration of exams is the issue of multiple choice versus open ended questions. Is one as good as the other? Do they achieve comparable results? I cannot claim complete open-mindedness on this point. It has been demonstrated to me that valid multiple choice tests can be devised that will indeed test for the subtle aspects of any discipline. I will simply stipulate that this is the case. Even so, except in the case of mathematical problems or the sciences, it is a rare multiple choice test that demonstrates the procedural knowledge that we should value. And where a correct answer *does* require significant thought and procedural knowledge, it cannot demand of the student inventive use of language to express ideas. And it is just this way of using language to express ideas that should be a significant outcome of education. With any choice-type test it is the test-maker who has had to struggle with the language. Getting the just-right syntax and vocabulary to formulate three or four plausible-sounding but incorrect choices is demanding brain work. I contend that this is what students should be doing.

Behind this perhaps unorthodox stand on examinations is my belief that exams should, like assignments, be learning experiences as well as evaluative mechanisms. If writing is a way to learn (see chapter 7), I'm in favor of using it to do just that, and at every opportunity. Undeniably, questions that require some facts *and* procedural knowledge, and then leave the student a blank space to be filled with her own words, present about as demanding an intellectual challenge as most of us would care to face. Prepared students who survive this trial will, indeed, "bear traces of the struggle." Intense concentration, under a little pressure, while wrestling with language, cannot but do something to the brain. Students have told me that certain aspects of biology will stick with them forever because they "discovered" them while taking an exam.

As noted, carefully designed "choice" tests can test any aspect of a discipline, but great care and diligence are demanded if they are not to degenerate into mere matching games. Beginning biology students, for example, will correctly match DNA with gene about 90 percent of the time. If you ask them to define gene without using DNA, or DNA without using gene, the success rate drops to about 2 percent. Clearly, the two terms are little more than nonsense sounds that they have learned to link. Matsuzawa (1996) has had great success in teaching chimpanzees to link symbols in this way. Learning to link symbols is a challenge not much different in kind from that given to pigeons that must learn to peck one spot for grain and a different spot for water. If our only expectation from an exam is a number from which a grade can be derived, the choice-type test is far and away the fastest, easiest, and most objective instrument to use. But if that's the only kind of challenge students face, they will continue to use their brains as temporary storage bins. They will be denied an excellent learning opportunity.

Clearly, reading, decoding, and grading pages of student handwriting puts a real burden on the grader. Evaluating student writing, like learning itself, just cannot be made easy. And while learning can become satisfying, exam grading has yet to acquire that characteristic for most of us. Encountering a clear and well-reasoned answer can lift one's spirits, but for the most part you just grit your teeth and plow on.

Feedback

Typically, students who have had three weeks to write a five-page paper will expect you to have read it critically and given it a grade by the next class period. Students prefer the shortest possible turn-around time on assignments and exams for a variety of reasons. The less noble reason is that they are quite unsure as to how they have done. Many persist in a belief that luck plays a major role in their performance, or at least in your evaluation of it. Even when they have procrastinated and botched an assignment, or come to an exam completely unprepared, some still have hope that they might have done well without knowing how. Living with uncertainty is torture. Uncertainty, however, is only one element that drives students' need for rapid turn-around.

Rapid feedback has merit well beyond satisfying student curiosity. This is especially so where the performance was particularly poor. When we write something it tends to stick in our heads whether it was right or wrong. The longer a garbled version of matters remains uncorrected in a student's head, the more difficult it becomes to eradicate it. Quick turn-around gives students an opportunity to clear up their thinking before the errors settle in for good. Some methods for quick feedback and its advantages will be taken up again in chapters 7 and 8.

Correcting Without Hurting

In spite of some severe criticism (Lerner 1996, Baumeister 1996), the theory that self-esteem is the prerequisite for learning still enjoys considerable support in many secondary schools. In practice, indiscriminately promoting self-esteem can encourage the notion that any opinion is as good as any other, even when the point in question is not a matter of opinion at all. A similar by-product is the belief that an answer or an assignment is as good as the effort that went into it. Teachers of new college students can find themselves facing students who have seldom if ever been told that they are simply wrong on an issue. They don't all take kindly to the news. Correcting error, like so much of dealing with new students, is a matter of some delicacy.

To say that a thing is to be done gently does not mean that it should not be done at all. Error must be corrected—why else are we here? The delicate part comes in distinguishing between *persons* being wrong, and *their answers* being wrong. This is clearly a semantic distinction without a real difference, but the entire point here is one of peoples' feelings. A student can be corrected in a way that makes her feel like a stupid person, or such that she feels like an OK person who happened to have a wrong idea about something.

Our human tendency to be kind face-to-face can fail us when we confront disembodied gibberish on paper. I would be ashamed to reveal some of the devastating things I've written, in the heat of the moment, on student exam papers. I now regret them all. When I'm about to let fly at some absurdity, I now ask myself, "How would I react if someone said that to me?" For most of us it's embarrassing, at the very least, to be detected in error. When we're set straight with a flourish it begins to look a lot like insult. So it is that a student can brood for days over a thoughtless comment on an assignment or exam. Our job, we need to remember, is to instruct students when they are in error, not to castigate them for it.

Timely feedback on student performance, even when that performance is a collection of errors, remains a desirable goal. Errors have less time to incubate and students see quick turn-around as a sign of care and concern on our part. And on those happy occasions when they have done well, students get a lift and are encouraged in their efforts if they see "good job," or "well done" on their work.

Carrots and Sticks

On the matter of feedback, a more general question arises: Which works better in the sense of improving performance, praise for what's good, or criticism of what's bad? I find this, again, to be an ill-formed question. The assumption that one or the other is consistently better forces us to abandon any benefit the other approach might offer. Unrelenting criticism identifies a teacher, in the eyes of students, as a nag and a scold. A steady diet of praise makes it the expected thing and not a cause for elation. Baumeister (1996) calls the bestowing of praise where it is not warranted, "a tragic mistake."

Praise is clearly called for where it is deserved. But it is equally true that there is merit in a critical evaluation. Lerner (1996) went back a hundred years to Alfred Benet for an insightful observation. Benet saw self-esteem as the normal and natural thing, and self-criticism as unnatural but necessary for intellectual development. This an eminently sensible position. If we could get students to criticize their own thinking, and correct their own errors, they would learn to be critical of what they hear, and of themselves, and in general become more circumspect without the hurt feelings engendered by external criticism.

This kind of critical wariness underpins a number of statements on the purpose of education. Harold Macmillan (quoting an anonymous Oxford don) ended a statement of the purpose of education by saying that an educated person "will know when a man is talking rot." Louis Schmier says that an educated person can "question the answers." Elsewhere I suggested that an education "relieves you of the burden of having to believe everything you are told" (Leamnson 1995). Bertrand Russell said that education protects one from the "seduction of eloquence." These formulations have something in common; they champion the critical mind over the credulous one.

Both Lerner (1996) and Baumeister (1996) conclude forcefully and explicitly that self-esteem and self-confidence provide no detectable improvement in learning, and both writers strongly suggest that the opposite is more probably true—intellectual accomplishment is the surest way to healthy self-esteem and self-confidence. All of which returns us to the challenging problem of fostering self-criticism in order to advance intellectual development. Later I'll suggest ways in which writing can be used to good advantage for this purpose. But whatever the vehicle or approach, error and befuddled thinking have to be pointed out. Having for the most part gone uncorrected in the past, some students will take offense at any suggestion that they are in error. Little can be done about that, except to gently desensitize them.

Were instructions available for such gentle desensitizing, they would probably be as useful as instructions on how to play the oboe. The best we can do is learn from any lapses in tact and press on. Corrections that students will certainly resent, as would anyone, are those that suggest that there is something wrong with *them* rather than with their beliefs. But, as noted earlier, few young college students see the distinction because so many of them are unaccustomed to criticism however it is directed.

To make corrections useful, and as painless as possible, avoid the pronoun *you*. Whether written or verbal, expressions like "your thinking is confused," "you've missed the point," or "you failed to take into account," are likely to be taken as rude at best and demeaning at worst. Comments that are more corrective than critical, such as, "the point here was . . ." or "the real situation is . . ." take more time and more words, but are also more likely to focus student thinking on the content and away from their egos.

Sometimes students (if they are invited and encouraged to do so) will bring graded writing assignments or exams to a teacher during office hours. For first-year students the point of a visit is usually to defend what they have written. If the teacher also takes a defensive stand, a potentially useful teaching/learning occasion can degenerate into mutual annoyance. Seldom does anything useful come from bickering with students. The best thing to do in these situations is to assume, or at least pretend to assume, that the student was indeed short changed. I have found the following protocol to work reasonably well, with the least hard feelings. Ask the student to verbalize or read what the assignment or the question had asked for. In many instances this task alone turns up a source of trouble. Words might be skipped over, or the student's paraphrase of the question might reveal a critical misunderstanding. When it's clear that the question is understood, have the student read aloud what he had written. I believe it is important that *they* do the reading and not you, and that it be done aloud. In the most desirable case, the student will see what's wrong without a word from you. If it becomes necessary to point out error, an interactive method is better than the didactic. But, as before, avoid use of the accusatory *you*. Focus attention on the writing and not the writer, almost as if it had been done by some third party. Questions like, "I wonder what *this* might mean?" (referring to a phrase or sentence) just might get the student to move a small step toward a self-critical attitude. "What did *you* mean by this?" on the other hand, can push the student into a defensive corner. Seeing graded work as a kind of independent entity that represents only fuzzy thinking enables student and teacher to collaborate in the repair. Typical students will defend *themselves* vigorously, but only a very few will persist in defending *error*.

As pointed out by Singal (1991) and others, students entering college in recent years have had their efforts at self-expression strongly reinforced. Self-expression is pretty much immune to outside criticism, so only a few high school students have had their thinking held up for scrutiny. Most of them don't much like the idea. Because scrutinizing and correcting are essential elements of college teaching, perhaps it's not surprising that freshmen and their teachers are often at loggerheads. Fortunately these young people are still pliable and resilient. So long as they don't really believe that you dislike them they'll bounce back and most of them will do what it takes to win your approval. Because reinforcement is essential for the establishment of new habits, don't fail to pile on the praise as they become more focused, logical, and self-critical.

Summary

These thoughts on teaching and learning (what teachers do and what students do) are based on my earlier suggestions as to what new students are like (not-quite-ready-for-all-this), what learning is (stabilizing, through repeated use, otherwise labile synapses), and what part language has in it all (converting fuzzy associations into firm verbalized ideas). For these reasons, nearly every practical suggestion made has in some way involved, or led to, students talking to their teachers and to one another. Study groups, in or out of the classroom, in-class recitations, and conferences are all effective in forcing verbalization of thought. New students will sometimes dislike talking to teachers if they assume every verbal interaction is a test and that they are expected to have the right answer and have it quickly. Persistence and patience are the only tools we have to break through this defensive position. A hundred years ago James (1904) wrote: "the extreme value of verbal recitation as an element of complete training may nowadays be too much forgotten." What would he have thought of today's "nowadays?"

Classroom teaching is demanding work. A roomful of students who are learning, or at least being inspired to learn, is in great part the result of effective teaching that has been consciously planned and carried out. But a *roomful* is probably too much to ask for. Nothing said in these or any other pages could so empower a teacher that his or her efforts would entice all students to learn at their capacity. What we might reasonably hope for would be a critical mass of converts. A few students who, through the teacher's encouragement, have come to believe that they have permission to verbalize their thoughts and questions will dramatically affect the classroom atmosphere. The invitation to vigorously engage the content within the classroom environment falls, nonetheless, on good soil and poor. Most, in fact, are not predisposed to engage in public discourse. A few even resist cooperative study in groups and are content to sit and listen. Still, *many more* will verbalize their questions and ideas in groups of four than will in a group of forty.

Setting small groups to work solving a problem or figuring out some complex relationship inevitably reveals errors of fact or logic that I would not have otherwise discovered until test time. Once a room gets noisy with the chatter of six or seven groups, hands start going up and I'm called first to one group and then to another to settle some debate or straighten out someone's thinking. At these times I get the feeling that I'm doing something very important.

7

WRITING AND OTHER
TECHNOLOGIES

If you are headed in the wrong direction, technology won't help you get to
the right place.

—Stephen Ehrmann

Teaching and technology have been connected at the hip for some time. So
much so in recent times that administrators increasingly link good teaching
to innovation and particularly to innovative uses of technology. The word
technology brings to most peoples' minds something with an electric cord
attached; and, indeed, enormous changes are taking place in schools at all
levels as a result of the nearly ubiquitous computer.

Meanings of words evolve with time and use, however, and technology
has lost much of its broad and utilitarian meaning of an invention to facilitate some process. How often do we think of books, for example, as technology? By definition, a *technology* is a means to an end. For students the
desired end should be learning, and for teachers it should be effective teaching. Every educational technology should be considered and evaluated in
light of its contribution to attaining one of these goals. We would also do
well to consider all technologies both from the point of view of students
(learning technologies) as well as that of teachers (teaching technologies)
because teaching and learning are, by my definitions, separable activities.

Writing: An Old and Potent Technology

Reading and writing are frequently referred to as skills by professionals in education. There can hardly be any arguing with that so far as it goes. Reading and writing do require practice and good practice does improve performance. However, dwelling on the skills aspect of reading and writing is not always productive. Page Smith's (1984) exasperation with the idea had about reached its limits when he wrote, "I'm bone-tired of the modern cant about learning skills, reading skills, language skills. A bleak world, this world of skills." The skills approach has also contributed to what Mike Rose called "the myth of transience" (in Russell 1991). That cryptic expression, unpacked, tells us a lot about some attitudes toward reading and writing. That deficiencies in reading or writing are transient problems that can be fixed with a remedial course or two is a fallacy that continues wastefully to drain time and resources. Both would be more wisely spent if we began to think of reading and writing as learning technologies. Such thinking does not deny the skill required for these activities, but it might chip away at the mistaken belief that they are transient problems. I suspect a number of teachers would re-think their methods if, instead of thinking of reading and writing as generic skills their students are supposed to have mastered, they saw their task to be the coaching of reading and writing in their particular disciplines.

The best I can say about reading was proposed earlier in the suggestion that students be required to paraphrase as a test of reading comprehension. Student writing, however, is accessible, and a sizable literature has sprung up on the topic of writing as a way to learn. William Zinsser's *Writing to Learn* (1988) and Toby Fulwiler's *Teaching with Writing* (1987) are both good sources for anyone not yet familiar with the idea.

The making of symbols (writing) and their interpretation (reading) are so linked and so fundamental that we give them a potent common name—literacy. It's difficult to imagine society, worldwide, drifting into nonliteracy. Employers still look for literate employees and will continue to do so for the foreseeable future. But it is useful to consider literacy not so much as a generic property of an individual, but more as one that maps onto some content. It is correct and useful to speak of historical literacy, economic literacy, chemical literacy, and so on.

Thinking of literacy as being to some degree content-specific might affect the way we teach. The psychology teacher who assumed his students were literate in the generic sense would also expect them to be psychologically literate once he had informed them of the facts. That teacher's approach will be notably different from one who believes that psychological literacy is something that he must teach, and his students practice, explicitly.

My experience has been that a majority of college teachers balk at this second approach—teaching content literacy. They perceive it as *teaching writing*, something they do not feel confident about doing, and something they believe should have already happened somewhere along the way. It becomes necessary here to make a fine distinction. There is a difference between the inability to write about a subject and the inability to construct valid and comprehensible sentences of any kind. Most of us encounter students, in their first year and later, who cannot write coherent sentences, no matter the topic. They have forgotten the subject by the time the verb comes along, or they decide to end it all before the verb arrives.

It's hard to know what to do with students who have found their way into college classrooms but cannot put any idea into a coherent sentence. We all await a longitudinal, broad-based study of the efficacy of remedial courses designed to address this problem. For now I have nothing to suggest to the college instructor faced with a preponderance of marginally literate (in the generic sense) students. More often the problem will be a lack of content literacy, and it is necessary that we distinguish this lack of content literacy from the generic kind.

Teachers who specialize in teaching writing as such use a number of technical terms to differentiate types of writing. I will borrow two of these here because they are useful in distinguishing between a literacy problem that is content-specific and one that is generic. *Experiential writing* as the term suggests, specifies writing that reports on, or comments on, one's experiences. "What I did on my summer vacation," is the classic example of experiential writing. *Referential writing* on the other hand, has as its subject not one's perception of, feelings about, or reaction to, some subject or event, but rather the subject or event itself. As a first approximation one can think of experiential writing as tending toward the subjective and referential writing as being more objective. The distinction is not absolute since both kinds of writing usually have some real thing or event as the subject. Referential writing, however, can be verified or refuted because it addresses issues, events, or situations that are accessible to all. So while my reaction to an event or situation, or my perception of it, is not refutable because it is personal and subjective, my account of that event or situation, or my understanding of it, is subject to error. Some students who do quite well at experiential writing can go all to pieces when required to write referentially, giving rise to their instructors' belief that they cannot write at all.

To estimate a student's understanding of economics or psychology, I would suspect that teachers in those fields would expect referential writing. Most teachers in most content areas are not so much interested in students' reaction to the topics as their understanding of it. When I refer to *writing* hereafter it will always mean referential writing—that which refers to some independently verifiable reality.

The Notion of Consonance

Before thinking about writing as a teaching technology, it will help to consider it first as a learning technology. A subtle and annoying aspect of writing to learn is that the learning does not happen automatically. This is not surprising, however, because there are no automatic or mindless processes that effect learning. Writing causes learning only when the writer has that intent, and even then only in an indirect way. Furthermore, the very idea that one can learn *through* writing is not a concept that students are particularly familiar with. Almost without exception they begin with one or the other of two wrong ideas. In the worst case, they do not see any connection at all between writing and learning. In that instance, the writing is little more than stenographic transcription. Beginning students usually see writing as a product, and if it can be produced with little or no thought, then why make it more strenuous than needs be? Our intent—that students use the assignment as a learning experience—is frequently subverted.

As noted before, assignments that require paraphrasing can, if done well, bring students to the point of understanding someone else's ideas, or the facts of the case, in preparation for writing. At that point, however, they can make a second mistake, albeit a less serious one; they assume that they have to know everything before they begin to write.

As most academics know, serious writing usually does mean having intent and arguments more or less in hand before starting. But we also know that not-yet-verbalized factual details are often nowhere to be found when it's time to put them into words. When Zinsser (1988) says that writing clarifies half-formed ideas, he is saying that the attempt to verbalize has exposed some fuzzy thinking. So it is that writing causes learning *indirectly*. What we thought was a clear and verbal idea wasn't at all. Attempting to write what is not yet verbal causes us to stop and think, or perhaps look up some facts.

I will introduce the word *consonance* here to indicate either of two agreeable states that a writer aspires to. The first instance of consonance would occur when we are at last assured that our mental state is in agreement with reality or accepted theory. The second occurs when we become content that the words we use accurately relate our mental state. Achieving consonance in both cases represents a high level of achievement in matters of academic content. The number of beginning college students who seriously try to make their writing consonant with either their mental state or the real world is not as large as we might hope.

Writing as a Teaching Technology

So if writing is a good but far-from-automatic learning technology for students, what can teachers do, other than assign it, that would make it a teaching technology? In a word, it means coaching. Beginning students may have no notion of how to read and write in a way that achieves what I am calling consonance. (I use this word for convenience. I doubt that any good would be accomplished by using the term with students.) At the most basic level, students must be convinced that stating as true what isn't true is simply not acceptable. Disabusing them of the notion that their opinion is all that is important might be a slow and painful ordeal, but it must be done. Wars, for example, must be fought in the right century and operas written by the real composers. Even so, a well-designed assignment will demand more than collecting the facts. Students don't always appreciate that truth, and they tend to be content when they have found some source. They sometimes see an assignment as a kind of treasure hunt, and once they discover the treasure they run with it and consider the hard work done. Perhaps it's our own overemphasis on looking things up that reinforces the treasure hunt approach.

One way to de-emphasize the *finding* part of an assignment and direct student attention to the *understanding* part is to make the finding part less labor intensive. Effective and challenging assignments that demand consonance at both levels can be designed such that only data or information from class notes and a textbook are needed. Explicitly pointing students toward easily accessible data demonstrates more clearly than words that it is the thinking and not the hunting that is important, and that nothing arcane or exotic is required to learn what needs to be learned.

Advanced upperclassmen certainly need to be skilled in searching out sources. It is, however, a relatively easily acquired talent compared with deciphering and digesting the content when it is discovered. Most upperclassmen seem to have learned this and they do not, as so many beginners do, believe that the job is done when the source has been found. Emphasizing the search, in the case of beginners, sends, I believe, the wrong signal.

I frequently hold an open forum in class about midway between the time an assignment is given and the date it is due. The intent is to answer questions on the content, or on just what is important, and anything else students care to bring up. Openly discussing an assignment that they have been working on directs their attention to the topic of the assignment and the importance of their knowing it well. It also reinforces the perception of the teacher as ally rather than adversary. A nice give-and-take session on an assignment in progress says that we're all in this together and the only real opponent is ignorance.

By far the best way to help students achieve consonance is to read and comment on an initial draft without grading it. I doubt that there is anything I do that is more appreciated by students and at the same time improves their understanding. Young people will sometimes produce pages of text all based on a colossal misunderstanding of things as they really are. Making them aware of their error (gently, as always), and giving them a second chance is much appreciated. Most make good use of the opportunity. I also extend a standing invitation to consult with me privately or by e-mail during the writing. A few do take advantage of the offer of a face-to-face conference, but so far not in such numbers as to make it impossible to do.

E-mail (which I'll discuss later) is a wonderful tool for making global comments on an assignment after the first draft. Certain problems crop up over and again, and a blanket e-mailing is a relatively painless way to get the message out. It greatly reduces the amount of commenting one needs to do on individual papers. Circling or bracketing text and marking it "S.E." (see e-mail) clues the writer that something is not quite right here and the details are in a group e-mail message. One of the striking and encouraging results of helping students with assignments has been my discovery that so many of them really do want to do well and sincerely appreciate our help.

The Effective Writing Assignment

If we believe writing to be a teaching technology, then we must further believe that there is something the teacher has to do beyond simply assigning writing. Implied or explicit in the following summary are the teacher activities that make writing a teaching technology.

1. *Give students a clear indication of audience.*

    I don't believe students should write with the teacher in mind as the audience, even though some highly respected student-oriented publications advocate it without hesitation. When students write *for* the teacher they will try to guess at what the teacher expects to see. They also assume that the audience, being the teacher, is not in need of instruction. They use big words and technical terms not because they explain anything, but because they think these are expected. A most effective audience, I have found, is the imaginary brother, sister, or friend, who is quite intelligent but uninformed about the topic of the assignment. The best student writing I've encountered has been done by those who were trying to relate what they've learned to someone else.

2. *Make the intent to teach a significant component of the assignment.*

    To capitalize on that last observation in 1. above, I now suggest, indeed urge, that students pretend, when they are writing, that they are teaching what they have learned for the benefit of some future reader. When teachers are called upon to teach an unfamiliar topic, we find ourselves reading and making notes with heightened attention. The same will be true for students, if we can just convince them to go along with the pretense.

3. *Provide an opportunity for revision.*

    As already noted, students really do appreciate, and profit from, a cost-free opportunity to get things straight in their heads. Referential writing is a novelty for some of them and they will not always bother to get their facts straight. The real benefit of a second draft, however, is the improvement they generally make. A single draft assignment is a little like a test—one chance to get it right. A two-draft assignment is a better learning experience because it provides a second chance to achieve consonance—to get their minds in synch with the facts and their writing in synch with their minds.

Few would argue with the position that writing can cause learning and that it is therefore good that students do it. But teachers should see writing as a teaching technology as well, because we are the ones who design the writing assignments, coach the students, and help them achieve consonance by way of our comments.

Surprising to some college teachers might be the observation that students can be more concerned with the opinions of their peers than of their teachers where writing is concerned. The Harvard Assessment Seminars (Light 1990–1992) relate the increased concentration and effort that students reported putting into their writing when they had been assigned to write for their classmates and had their efforts photocopied and distributed or made available for everyone to read. This is clearly not something that can be done in large classes, but, having been subjected to this attention-focusing technique, I recommend it highly wherever it can be done.

More Technologies

Technologies, as noted, are tools for getting something done. Most teaching technologies, beyond writing, have something to do with access. By that I mean the making public of private information. Probably the oldest and still most-used teaching technology is the chalk board. There may be a classroom somewhere that doesn't have one, but I doubt that any but the most relentlessly progressive teacher would be long content teaching there. Competently used, the chalkboard gives public access to whatever the teacher, or a student, has in mind. This humble old technology also facilitates a technique that is almost indispensable in mathematics, science, engineering, and helpful in most other disciplines; that being the gradual and stepwise development of systems and arguments. At the 1997 meeting of the *Society for Teaching and Learning in Higher Education* (STLHE), during a session devoted to technologies, one soft-spoken professor commented that he really liked his chalkboard because he could "show process as well as product."

There followed a lusty burst of applause—embarrassing to the organizers, who clearly had loftier things in mind. There are, to be sure, animation programs for computers that achieve the same end, but the teacher is not really in control of the content unless he or she is quite proficient in writing animation programs. And the chalkboard has one more almost mystical property that I'm constantly amazed at. Even the most indifferent student seems compelled to copy into notes anything that is written on the board. There is, on the other hand, a notable tendency to simply stare at a computer terminal. Finally, there is Clifford Stoll's (1995) amusing description of people about to give a presentation via electronic media and their nervousness, if not near-panic, from fear that something is going to go wrong. (The CEO of Microsoft, Bill Gates, it seems, suffered just this embarrassment during his first unveiling of Windows '98.) Stoll contrasts that with a chalk-talk, where "you can keep going even if the chalk breaks."

Inventions for making information public comprise books, recordings, and many methods of visual display. Because these technologies can also be used to entertain, or even misinform, none of them can be used indiscriminately. For teaching/learning technologies, the medium should not be the message. A number of new college students come to us practiced in doing assigned school work without engaging the learning centers in their brains. These students can sometimes do a writing assignment without learning anything substantial by it. If they can bypass the learning intent of an active process like writing, they will also be able to subvert the more passive format of most high technology.

High Technology

We come, then, to things with electric cords. Those of us my age will have to be excused if our pulse rates fail to race at each new breakthrough in educational technology. There have been so many. If there has been a consistent pattern in technological advances, and teaching innovation in general, it has been that the new thing is in no way comparable to any previous advance, and the promised improvement in learning is just around the corner. Computers, journalists warned breathlessly, were about to unleash a wave of high school graduates so advanced that their college instructors would be struggling to keep up. Most of us are still awaiting this new challenge.

We are approaching, if we haven't reached it, the point where our college students will have been born within the personal computer era. Certainly some have had one or more computers in their classrooms since the first grade. The effect has not yet shown up on any of the common instruments for gauging learning. Electronic technology has effected significant and undeniable changes in what (some) teachers do, what (some) students do, and how (some) courses are taught. It will take a large study, such as Astin's (1993) survey of what makes a detectable difference during college to determine how much learning has improved during the high technological period, and to what extent it can be attributed to the use of higher technology.

Now that I have created the clear impression that I'm a crusty old Luddite, I'll try to persuade you that this is not the case. I am, in fact, a gadget person. I love tools of all kinds, as well as disc and tape players, television and VCRs, and indeed, computers. I own two or three of almost everything. The earlier nay saying was only to emphasize again my recurring theme—learning takes place in students' brains and only they can make it happen. In fact, my caveats are mild compared to those of Neil Postman (1992) who speaks to the hearts of many a dedicated and serious teacher, and who is openly and deeply pessimistic about the effects of increased reliance on high technology. And my perception is almost upbeat compared to the dim view taken by Stoll (1995), an avowed computer geek who sees the "computer solution" as the modern equivalent of snake oil. I am simply in agreement with the major argument of both, that social problems—including explicitly those of education—will not be solved by technology. As suggested by Ehrmann's quotation that opens this chapter, technology can get you someplace quickly and with minimum expenditure of energy, but technology cannot tell you where you ought to be.

What then of teaching? Assuming the destination is well in hand, how does the teacher use technologies of such power and potential? This is a pivotal question, because the idea that students, on their own, will use technology to educate themselves is as believable as David Sarnoff's prediction on the future effects of television. He said, in 1939, "It is probable that television drama of high caliber and produced by first-rate artists will materially raise the level of dramatic taste of the nation." So much for foreseeing the course of social evolution. Just as television evolved to accommodate user expectations, so will most consumer technologies.

If technology is to improve education it will be because teachers who truly understand learning take matters in hand and decide just what that technology will be used to do. And the power and influence of such teachers can be significant. Ehrmann (1995) relates a study he and his associates conducted at Reed College. They chose Reed because students there had all had personal computers for some years. The relevant question put to faculty and students was, what difference had the computers made in teaching and learning? The answers hardly suggested anything spectacular, but they were remarkably similar. Teachers had lost their previous reluctance to ask students to redo their written work when improvement was needed, and students had come to see the value of revision. A few teachers had even coined a name for improving through revision. They called it *DIATing*—Do It Again, Thoughtfully. Remarkably, this state of affairs had come about without benefit of any central or pre-planned strategy. Teachers acting independently had come to see the potential for word processing to improve learning. Most of us have come to see the benefits of word processing. It doesn't replace anything that students must do to learn by writing, but used properly it does what all good tools do—it speeds up the physical labor part and makes it more satisfying.

E-mail

Another wonderful aspect of computer technology, one that probably needs no introduction, is electronic mail, or e-mail. It's a rare college campus that has not gotten connected to the Internet and so made it possible for faculty and students to "talk" to anyone who is also connected, anywhere in the world. But this convenience is also a great teaching tool—one with some surprising and beneficial collateral effects.

My home institution is blessed with a friendly and responsive support group for faculty computer use. Usually within a day of my request, user I.D.s for all the students in all the sections I teach show up in my e-mail. Within seconds I can make a distribution list that enables me to send the same message to everyone on that list. A few days later copies of passwords, log-in instructions, and anything else students need to get started come by campus mail. I send out a test message, usually something informal and chatty, and request a response to see if everyone is logging in. And here I have to take issue with "common knowledge." That most students will come to college so computer literate that the faculty will be going to them for help, is just so much loose talk. There are such students (I rely on several) but they remain a very small fraction of the total. Computer proficiency comes highly concentrated in a few students, and these, not surprisingly, get a lot of press. There are in fact a surprising number of new college students who simply don't know what to do with a computer, and a small number who hate or fear them and will have nothing to do with them. Alongside these twenty-year-olds with a fear and loathing of computers are some sixty-year-olds who can go anywhere the mouse can take them. Whether anyone is a techie or not is in the genes I think. That it's all a matter of age is patent nonsense.

So if you are "into" computers, be prepared to do a little hand-holding with a few of the youngsters—it's not true that they all come predisposed to "do" technology. If you, as teacher, happen not to be predisposed, well, remember the part about brain synapses and learning—you're never too old. Besides, there are some neat things you can do with computers that really help students learn.

E-mail, for example, produces some unexpected results. E-mail tends to resemble talking more than it does literate discourse. Many students (and others) are not conversant with the e-mail editor function, and messages can be strange-looking indeed, with words abandoned part way through and started over, typos ignored or followed by "(sorry)." For some reason, perhaps the strain of pressing the shift key, more and more messages are coming without any capitalization, including the first person singular pronoun. All of which is to say that you may have to do some reading between the lines and sometimes a little interpolating to find the message within the e-mail message. But there is an up side to the pell mell way students tend to write e-mail messages. While chattering away they will say things, or ask questions, that they would never say or ask in public and for which they would not make the trip to your office. Dumb questions don't seem quite so dumb when they are typed secretly on a keyboard. Sometimes students' normal conversational speech is so cluttered with "like's" and "y'know's" that they really cannot formulate in literate speech what it is they want to say. With a keyboard, ample time, and the assurance that nothing will be seen until they finally decide to send it, they sometimes make more sense in e-mail than they do in person. And that works both ways. A question that comes by e-mail does not demand that I start talking whether I'm ready or not. I can think, reread, try something, throw that out, try again, concentrate on being nice, and in general produce a considered response which, again, will not be seen until I'm satisfied and sent it off.

A tough writing assignment or a test in the offing usually brings on an increase in e-mail traffic. If I begin to see a trend, or a common problem, I can formulate a clarification, or a quick review, and sent it to the whole class. I always get a few "thank you" notes when I do this. In summary, e-mail is an easily acquired habit with a big payoff at little cost. And it is not, as sometimes claimed, a cold, distant, or impersonal way to communicate. Getting e-mail is like getting regular mail. What could be nicer?

You can also get connected, through e-mail, to a nearly unimaginable number of newsgroups and lists. *The Chronicle of Higher Education, Change,* and other educational publications are a good source for addresses and instructions for getting connected. If, for example, you want to join a discussion on high technology in education, or just look in on one (*lurking* in tech-talk), address an e-mail message to LISTPROC@LIST.CREN.NET and for the message type only: "subscribe aahesgit" (without the quotation marks) followed by your first name and your last name (not your e-mail name/address). Some instructions will come back on how to post messages to all subscribers, and how to get off the list if you want.

Still Higher Technology

Geohegan (1995) reported that any new educational technology or application is rapidly adopted, or tested out by 10 percent to 15 percent of college faculty. The remaining 85 percent take a wait-and-see stance or never notice. The 10 to 15 percent represent the true techies who may use technology simply because it's there. For the "early adopters," as they are called, the presumption seems to be that the technology will improve teaching/learning and the challenge is one of implementation. The technology at this level tends toward making connections. Websites on the Internet provide almost unimaginable access. Those who are inclined can construct their own homepage and these can become quite elaborate and useful. The syllabus, assignments, comments on readings, class notes (for those who believe them beneficial), sample problems, material downloaded from other sources, chatrooms, student question pages, and more can be put on a home page. Teachers and students who are into computers take readily to this technology. The growing interest in connecting campuses to remote locations by way of two-way communication will result in more distance learning and consequent modifications of teaching methods. But numerous books on these topics are already on the shelves so the nuts and bolts of these higher technologies will not be pursued here.

One small reservation regarding some of the higher technologies is prompted by the real possibility that students who are not fond of technology (a significant fraction, I suspect) will not participate optimally, or will see it as just more busywork. If considering the individual differences between students is a good thing, such consideration should extend to their propensity for using gadgets. What this means for teachers is that our job of encouraging the use of learning methods, such as writing assignments and study groups, will have to include the use of newer technologies as well—at least for some. What is true of learning processes in general is also true of the higher technological methods. They do not substantially reduce the effort and persistence that are part and parcel of effective teaching.

Websites and other ways of connecting campuses, libraries, and organizations have been correctly praised for increasing access to an almost unbelievable level. Access, in turn, has been considered an unmitigated good. The conclusion, however, that increased access on its own will lead to increased learning remains undemonstrated and is almost certainly false. Jonathan Schell (1996), writing in *The Atlantic Monthly*, was pulling no punches when he said, "It's a paradox of our time that the increase in information has been paralleled by an increase in ignorance." What students need in order to learn has always been available in modern times. That the amount of information available has been the limiting element in student learning is a position difficult to defend. That "more" is now easily accessed is, of course, obvious. But along with increased data and ease of access come some unanticipated problems. As just one example, the many stories of young children being approached by pedophiles by way of the Internet are alarming a lot of parents.

As this section is being written, two news items remind us that not everything we see on a website is information, and that more is not always better. It was announced, solemnly, in the United States Congress that comedian/entertainer Bob Hope had died. Hope was at about that time enjoying breakfast and understandably surprised by the news. It seems someone found this information on an Associated Press website and figured their congressman would score a small *coup* by being the first to announce it.

Concurrently the Central Intelligence Agency was being taken to task for not having discovered that India was about to test nuclear explosive devices. It transpired, shortly after, that the CIA was spending about 95 percent of its information budget on hardware—satellites, computers, and the like. There was so little money left to hire analysts that only about 6 percent of the data collected was receiving study. Satellite photos of the reaction site had been there all along, but not available was a human brain able to analyze them.

No matter how much data (true or otherwise) becomes available, learning will still result only when some person with a well-structured brain sorts it out and makes sense of it.

Pleiotropic Effects

The ripples of technological backlash appear shortly after the hoopla that ushers in the technology. Warnings, about computers in particular, continue to appear in books (Postman 1992, Stoll 1995) and in the press. Todd Oppenheimer (1997) reviews the many promises of technology going back to 1922 when Thomas Edison predicted that movies would replace books in the classroom. As Larry Cuban (1986) noted in his history of educational technology, none of the promised dividends of investment in educational technology (other than the printing press) have so far materialized. But hope springs eternal. And in truth, there has never before been anything quite like the computer. The question that presses on us is, what do we do with it? For young people with a natural predilection for gadgets, no encouragement to *use* the computer is needed. But, paradoxically, what they use it *for* often depends on their level of education.

Some senior students descended on my office one day looking for help on something called "phage display library," a somewhat technical subject another teacher had alluded to. My personal recollection of the phenomenon was dim so we set about looking in books and journals. We had made some progress when someone suggested that it might be on the Web. One of the techies went off like a shot and in minutes had a printout of *someone's* understanding of the subject. The website entry was highly condensed, but fortunately filled in what we needed for a reasonably complete picture. These experienced and highly motivated students are the people who can truly benefit from computers, websites, and any other technology that becomes available. They are discriminating and critical and know when someone is talking rot. The question that presses on us is, did they get to be that way by using technology or did their education enable them to take advantage of the flood of information that technology makes available?

The easy answer is that they went together, each reinforcing the other. But that is not a satisfying answer. Such an answer lets us sidestep the issue of causality. And in practice many teachers will, wittingly or not, approach their tasks believing either that the new technologies will cause learning, or that learning is a prerequisite for making sense of the information we are virtually drowning in.

I suspect the best teaching will be done not by those who take one position or the other and never deviate, nor by those who attempt a middle-of-the-road course. I believe it will be done by teachers who can accurately determine just when high technology can facilitate learning and when it is that some intellectual capital is needed to cope with the technology. Instructors who plan their teaching in this analytical way will also provide their students with some welcome variety in and out of the classroom.

Pleiotropy, in biology, is a term used to designate multiple effects emanating from a single cause. The gene for sickle cell anemia, for example, causes reduced oxygen dispersal to cells, but it also causes a seemingly unrelated effect, a reduced susceptibility to malaria.

Teaching spawns pleiotropic effects constantly. One's intent might be to teach anthropology, but students pick up language habits, bits of psychology, values, and who knows what else from the teaching. It might be well to end this chapter with some philosophical considerations of possible pleiotropic effects of higher technology. This is unexplored territory, but we can take a lead from the observations of Ong (1982) and others who have studied the impact of writing on human culture. The ability to fix one's words and thoughts in permanent symbols was certainly a remarkable invention— high technology for the times. Who could have anticipated that merely making permanent records would affect the way people spoke and thought? Most researchers agree that literacy pushed thinking past the specific and concrete toward the general and abstract, which in turn led to extensive categorization and the syllogistic logic we now value so highly.

It's an open question whether or not the new modes of information transfer are going to have an effect, eventually, on the way people think. Will hypertext and hotlinks, for example, speed up certain mental processes or simply bypass them? Will the ability to move effortlessly to topics that the programmer found related help to focus attention or will it encourage electronic wool-gathering and disrupt concentration? These are areas for heady speculation, but they bring to the fore the question of language—how much we value it now or will value it in the future. Will language continue to be the currency of education? Assuming hopefully that it will be, we would do well to monitor the effects of technology on language. As was the case with literacy, we can't really anticipate the possible pleiotropic effects of technology as they might affect language use and thinking. Postman (1995) draws attention to a truth that is underappreciated when he says, "Technological change is not additive; it is ecological. A new technology does not merely add something; it changes everything." Jane Healy (1990) seems not to be terribly optimistic when she quotes a *Forbes* magazine article (August 27, 1984) as follows: "In the end it is the poor who will be chained to the computer; the rich will get teachers."

8

FINAL THOUGHTS

But above style, and above knowledge,
there is something, a vague shape like
fate above the Greek gods. That some-
thing is power.
                         —Alfred N. Whitehead

As suggested in the Highet quote that began chapter 1, teaching new college students is indeed a matter of interfering with their lives. If my definition of learning has validity, then students who learn will have permanently altered their brains. Until further cognitive changes take place later in life, college graduates will find those neural paths stabilized by college learning firing away spontaneously to help cope with new situations. And if my definition of teaching hits the mark, we, their teachers, will have had a significant part in, perhaps some responsibility for, what neural patterns became hardwired and stable.

Astin (1993) has demonstrated that college graduates profit in all areas from their college work (with the possible exception of mathematics, where, on average, there may be a small loss in ability). College graduates, however, are those who persisted. For typical colleges those who persist constitute about half of those who matriculated. The majority of students who drop out for academic reasons do so in the first or second year.

Teachers of first-year students will probably have a good feel for why so many drop out. The difficulties new students exhibit because of an inadequate preparation are frequently lumped and referred to as "the transition problem." As noted earlier, most schools have long recognized the problem and most faculty would agree that acculturating students to the college experience and giving them good teaching, advice, and counseling would help them adjust to the new environment. But as Weingartner (1992) noted, *orientation, advising,* and *counseling* have, through "linguistic deterioration," become codified and bureaucratized to the point where they are more symbolic than real. How effective, for example, can orientation to college work be if it ends before students enter their first class? And counseling, in its ordinary and nonclinical meaning, need not be limited to a central agency and turned to only as a last resort. All of these student needs are really ongoing and should be the concern of all of us. For the new students, "being their teacher" means considerably more than teaching their classes.

Teaching While Not Teaching

New students' real introduction to the academic rules and rigors of college life comes in the courses they take. Ideally, every faculty member who teaches first-year students would be an orientation leader. As Joseph Lowman (1995) said, "Students need affection from college teachers, not as parents or lovers, but as adults who approve of them as learners and persons." First-year students may be walking around with a need they can't quite put into words—the need for a grownup friend. Young people might not, however, seek or expect approval and friendship from a stranger or a functionary. They might find the just-right person in student services, or through formal advising or counseling. But their teachers are the adults they encounter regularly and frequently. They have ample time to watch what we do, what we say, and how we react. They do, at some level, get to know us. It should not be surprising if some of them pick a teacher to be their adult friend.

As noted earlier, interests and values are often "caught" from teachers. Teachers themselves are seldom aware that this is going on, but that kind of inspiring might be thought of as unconscious teaching (realizing of course that such an expression is inconsistent with my earlier definition of teaching). More properly we would say that students learn from us even when we are not teaching.

One of the surest ways to show our concern for students is to be available to them. I would have to agree here, that college students can be almost childishly self-centered in their expectations regarding your availability. We have all heard the complaint, "she's *never* in her office." That complaint might well be an extrapolation from a single visit, possibly while that teacher was in class. But putting the extreme cases aside, it is in everyone's best interest to bend over backwards in trying to accommodate students who want to talk. Sending students away with the recommendation that they come back during posted office hours is certainly legal, but it sends a discouraging message.

If you want to go that extra mile, few things delight students more than one of their teachers showing up for their recital, their part in a play, their tennis match, or soccer game. Remember that the research on the topic of student/teacher interaction in college has already been done. Both Astin (1993) and Light (1990) found that getting connected with faculty was the number one contributing factor toward a successful and rewarding college experience, followed closely by interaction with peers on academic matters.

A lot of learning goes on outside the classroom. Lowman (1995) suggests that most of it does. When students are struggling with something outside of class time, either individually or in groups, they dearly appreciate having you available in a pinch. With more of them becoming comfortable with e-mail, my new mail file has an increasing number of requests for help, or for clarification, or to settle some argument. I try always to respond as soon as a question on coursework comes in. Even when I'm not on campus I check the e-mail from home periodically and always respond immediately to student questions.

All out-of-class interactions with students, face-to-face or electronic, should be personal and friendly. As Page Smith (1990) said, "Teachers who love their students are of course by that very fact teaching their students the nature of love, although the course may in fact be chemistry or computer science." He thoroughly endorses out-of-class contacts between students and faculty, "because they reveal something to the student about reality that can, I suspect, be learned no other say. Such contacts demonstrate that ideas are 'embodied.' They do not exist apart from a person, remote or near at hand, who enunciates, who takes responsibility for them by declaring them, by speaking about them." Or in the words of Woodrow Wilson, "We shall never succeed in creating this organic passion, this great use of the mind . . . until [we] have utterly destroyed the practice of merely formal contact . . . between teacher and pupil."

How Am I Doing?

Any philosophy of teaching will have as one of its elements a more or less explicit notion of just what it is you want to achieve by teaching. That your students learn something useful would certainly be a desirable outcome. But setting goals is the easy part. How can you tell if you are achieving what you set out to do? While that seems a simple question it is one of the most contentious ones in the business of education. Every method has its detractors. In some of the disciplines, standardized tests are available and these would appear to be an objective way to see how much your students have learned. But standardized tests put you and your students at the mercy of someone else's idea of what's important or how much is important. They are frequently so formidably comprehensive that they depress both students and teacher. Both may come away feeling that class time and study time have been wasted. In the worst cases they lead to a grim, relentless drive to prepare for the test.

But, for the sake of argument, let us imagine a perfect measuring instrument that gave realistic evidence of how much your students had learned. Whether the results were good or bad, the question remains: To what extent did your teaching contribute to the result? What was once thought to be an obvious answer—"ask the students"—has become a hotly debated issue. Student course/teacher evaluations have been studied on the basis of sound theory, statistical reliability, and validity in literally thousands of reports. While most of these are favorable, the vast majority of the teachers being so evaluated are not in the business of doing and publishing the kind of research that supports the practice. It is from that quarter that one hears the muttering. When the *Chronicle of Higher Education* (January 16, 1998) published an article on course evaluation by students, their online forum, Colloquy, crackled for weeks afterward with energetic claims from both sides of the question. A sample of some claims and counterclaims can be found in articles by Paul Trout (1997) and by Wendy Williams and Stephen Ceci (1997). Both articles state opinions and are accompanied by responses and rejoinders from those of differing beliefs. When faced with evidence both for and against a claim, it's best to withhold judgment. So I will suggest here only two small items to consider when wondering what to make of your course/teacher evaluations.

Many student response forms use a numbered scale, say one to five, to evaluate aspects of the course or the teaching. Because twenty, thirty, a hundred or more evaluations might be submitted, results on each item are reported as averages. An unwarranted faith is put in these averages. Clearly, thirty students picking "3" on an item is in no way comparable to fifteen picking "1" and fifteen picking "5," even if the average is "3" in both cases. Keep an eye on the standard deviation. A nearly random spread of numbers might be more indicative of emotional responses than considered ones.

When student evaluations are in the form of written responses to open ended questions, you can learn a considerable amount about the match between your intent and student perception. Again, the standard deviation problem, while not quantitative in this instance, needs to be considered. It's probably safe to ignore both the gushing paean and the vitriolic diatribe. Since both respondents were talking about the same teacher in the same course, that kind of reporting probably says more about the individual students than it does the teacher.

In written evaluations, look for comments that are similar on a good fraction of the papers and address fairly specific activity or behavior of yours. If you see, "he talks to the blackboard" four or five times, then you are probably talking to the blackboard.

Unless they are true, periodic comments like "he doesn't like students" or "she doesn't like teaching" need not upset anyone unduly. These are clearly judgments being made on very indirect evidence and say little about anyone's teaching or the students' learning. Even so, if such comments become commonplace, it may mean that the teaching persona needs tending to. In fact, I would consider it a serious matter if students in numbers persisted in the belief that a teacher did not like them, not because it says anything about the teaching, but because it can have a detrimental effect on students' learning and on their attitude toward the discipline. That this perhaps should not be so does not negate the fact that it is so. Students want to like their teachers and they expect us to like them.

"Boring" is the catchall adjective when students don't like what's going on but can't quite articulate just what they don't like. Certainly we should react to a chorus of such responses. But the reaction should not be a *direct effort* to not be boring. There are endless ways to keep students from being bored, but only a handful might be educational. If your predominant mode of teaching leans toward the innovative, such as dividing the content into a set of problems or projects to be worked on in teams, pay attention to *all* comments, good and bad, that address that technique. (I would caution, however, against specifically asking students to comment on any particular method or technique. In spite of our best efforts, we send signals and are likely to get the response we are looking for.)

To make sense of written comments one also has to know a little of the teen vocabulary of the day. The word *fun* is often used for any sensation of satisfaction or any activity that did not bore them. One of my students even reported finding exams "fun." What she meant, it turned out, was that they were original and challenging and she liked that kind of mental workout. Similarly, being "stressed" may not mean anything so clinically alarming as it sounds. It might mean only that they had to pay close attention and spend an unusual amount of time outside of class on coursework.

The reliability of student evaluations could be calibrated if we had a standard and direct way to measure teaching effectiveness. We don't have that, so faith in student evaluations is just that, a matter of faith. Because student learning is a goal most would agree on, it would seem that it would be a simple matter to test the correlation between how much is learned (in the sense of value added) and student evaluations. This has been done of course, but the results are puzzling. Stephen Ceci (Williams and Ceci 1997) was able to raise his evaluations compared to controls on all items (including the value of the textbook, which was the same in both cases) by a clever acting scheme. While *his* scores went up dramatically, student scores on exams were unaffected. Rodin and Rodin (1972) found, more puzzling still, that students' achievement showed an *inverse* correlation with evaluations of their instructors.

We might be forgiven uncertainty about the whole endeavor when we recall the famous "Dr. Fox Lecture," (Naftulin et al. 1973) where excellent ratings were given to a skillful actor who read with enthusiasm and flair, a completely meaningless lecture. More recently Ambady and Rosenthal (1993) showed that student volunteers watching a thirty second soundless videoclip of a teacher in action gave that teacher ratings nearly identical (correlation at the .76 level) to those given by that teacher's real students at semester's end.

After serving on many committees for evaluating colleagues for merit pay, contract renewal, tenure, and promotion, and after having read many reports and several metaanalyses on student evaluations, I remain unsure of just what it is student evaluations tell us about teaching. Therefore I have only one tentative suggestion. It is probably, in the case of first-year students, not a good idea to sculpt one's teaching to achieve the highest student ratings. These college beginners tend to use their level of comfort as a yardstick to measure their teachers. I suspect that few experienced college teachers would believe that much serious learning goes on when students are in a state of maximum comfort.

Innovations

What to do when all is not going well? How do you *know* when all is not going well? These are matters again on which there is no real consensus. Some instructors ask their students for an anonymous and informal mid-course evaluation. These are subject to the same uncertainties as the formal evaluations, but, as before, one can look for common elements such as the respondents being consistently bored. Repeated eye-contact is also a good way to see if students are "with you." Short quizzes that require writing provide a clue as to how much is being assimilated. If you are the only one doing any talking I would suspect that a course correction might be in order. Sometimes it's just a gut reaction that tells the perceptive teacher that something is not quite right.

Changing what you've been doing, particularly if you've been doing it a long time, is both risky and unsettling. But if you believe something new is warranted, the first thing to remember is that change is *not* synonymous with improvement. Virtually any change in teaching methods will elicit some response on the part of students, usually favorable because they appreciate a break in any routine. (The well-known Hawthorne effect.) Noting a positive response to any innovative method, we are tempted to believe that we have found "the solution." But, as Jacques Barzun (1991) warned, teaching and learning are not problems for which we have yet to find a solution, they are simply activities that are difficult to do well. Innovations that make everyone's life easier may well increase the comfort level, but these need to be monitored scrupulously to ensure that the kind of learning we want is not being sacrificed.

Learning is a word that attracts adjectives like a magnet. Constructive learning, inquiry learning, discovery learning, active learning, problem-based learning, service learning, cooperative learning, outcomes-based learning, and project-based learning are some of the varieties that have been designed, researched, and published. To someone new to this literature it might appear that there are many *kinds* of learning. But it is not learning that has multiple forms, but the methods and techniques used to elicit it. These all aspire to the same end. As one colleague mused, the important distinction is not between *this* kind of learning and *that*, but between learning and not learning. If there is any mistake in the application of methods or approaches it would be in believing that some technique held the key to solving the problem of education. O. P. Kolstoe's thoughts on finding "the solution" are not exactly mainstream, but there is wisdom there worth considering. He wrote: "The successful teacher is apt to be the one who honestly faces the fact that communication is a very personal thing between each instructor and each student. Universal [alternatives to this] simply are myths pursued by naïve teachers and technology hucksters" (1975). Joseph Lowman apparently agrees as he quoted this passage in *Mastering The Techniques of Teaching* (1995) where he also wrote: "Do not let this [his] book's emphasis on college teaching as artistic performance in an interpersonal arena obscure the fact that the ability to read and write critically has long been the fundamental skill of an educated person, and *this is developed largely through individual efforts outside the classroom* (emphasis added.)" All of this to make the point that no technique or approach is going to achieve anything lasting unless it inspires students to continue in their individual and personal struggles with the language.

Research on what the brain is doing when it learns has led me to look for certain common elements in the many innovative methods being championed—elements that might lead to the synaptic stabilizations in the brain that constitute learning. When collaborative efforts, for example, are at the very heart of the innovation being described there is almost always a line or two reminding us that students must be *individually* responsible. This is soft language and glosses a little the truth that students must spend some time with books, notes, and their own thoughts and words if learning is to happen. Be wary of activities that either remove individual responsibility or bypass the need for language acquisition. Pelikan (1992) suggested that students might learn a third of what they do learn in college from their teachers, another third from one another, but the remaining third from private study in the laboratory or library.

But we must face it. Sometimes the problem with a class of new students can be traced to the fact that far too many college teachers talk too much of the time in the classroom. But improving our pedagogy does not mean totally abandoning a style and swinging pendulum-like to an opposite extreme. Stephen Brookfield (1990) relates his early teaching experiences after a preparation that, in his words, viewed lecturing as "domineering, authoritarian and disrespectful of students' dignity." He vowed he would not do it, and taught his courses as "discussions" wherein the students developed solutions to the problems of the discipline. He experienced a small rebellion because even the students recognized that their "discussions" were rambling, unfocused, and unsupported by any intellectual capital to draw on. They were experiencing exactly what Eble (1988) warned of. "Students resent discussions that are really lectures, but they also resent discussion classes in which they are expected to profit solely from the half-baked ideas of other students, with no correctives from facts, experiences, and hard exacting thought." Brookfield's students were irritated by a teacher who never told them what he knew. His advice, many years later: "judge whether or not to use a particular method by the extent to which it helps people learn" (1990). No one has ever said it better.

One has to be quite honest about judging how much talking is too much and how much is just right. Unless you are an absolute virtuoso, most first-year students will start drifting after twenty to twenty-five minutes of uninterrupted talk. They can, in fact, stay focused for considerably longer periods, but only if they are being entertained, or if they get somehow involved in the goings on—involvement that goes beyond watching and listening.

Summarized here, and including several ideas from previous chapters, are some alternatives to long stretches of lecturing.

1. DIALOGUE WITH STUDENTS.

Even in large classes it is possible to engage students, a few each period, in discourse that goes beyond one word answers to set questions. At the beginning of a period this technique alerts students to where they are and what they are about. Used consistently, it gets a good number to come in prepared. It also apprises the teacher of misconceptions left over from a previous session.

2. THE INTERRUPTED LECTURE.

For beginning college students, two short lectures in the same period are better than one long one. A mid-period break resets their attention-span clocks while it provides an opportunity for group study, review, more dialogue, or a quiz, preferably after a short communal study session.

3. PROGRESS REPORT ON AN ASSIGNMENT.

Students are more likely to have questions or comments on something they have spent some time working on. Those who are not putting it off until the last minute will probably welcome a discussion on problems they've encountered on an assignment in progress.

4. GIVE STUDENTS A CHANCE TO INSTRUCT.

Letting students present to the class is an idea that is highly recommended, but with qualifications. Some subjects lend themselves to the practice while others do not. Business courses are good places to assign a team project report, and literature courses provide an opportunity for public readings or the presentation of a scene from a play. Given ample preparation time, students take these presentations very seriously. Astin (1993) found that they also stick in students' minds and they recall them as important elements in their education.

5. DEBATE THE DEBATABLE.

The admonition to never discuss politics or religion stems from the truth that these are areas where there are no answers that can be convincingly demonstrated to be better than others. Should your discipline bristle with debatable issues, why not let the students have at it? It's an excellent opportunity to coach in the area of marshaling valid arguments and substantiating claims.

Seeing is Believing

Few things tell you more about your teaching and the effect it is having than seeing yourself in action. The opportunity might be available if your institution has a teaching center or faculty development center. Such programs are variable in the kinds and quality of services they provide, but if you can get a trained video camera operator to tape several classroom sessions, you will have a valuable aid available for study. A trained camera-person is just about essential here, because it's important that they know when to follow you, when to focus on one student or a large group, when to look for a broad view and when to zoom in on you, or the chalkboard, or one student. It's also highly instructive to have someone else view the tape with you.

I once watched a tape of my teaching with about half the students who were in the class when the tape was made (these were all juniors or seniors). A quite remarkable and unexpected thing happened as we watched. The students (a wholly uninhibited lot) began making comments almost immediately. What was remarkable was that their comments always referred to me as "he" or "him," and never as "you," even though I was sitting in their midst. Representative of what I heard were, "He's wearing that green shirt again." "Notice how his arms flop around when he's making up stuff?" "Let's count how many times he pulls his beard." "Oh, here's where he does clamp proteins. Did anybody understand that?" (Chorus) "Not a word." "Look, he's stuck again," while I, on the monitor, stood staring at something I'd put on the board and obviously couldn't remember why.

It was, in short, a revelatory experience. It reminded me somewhat of the "visitor's reports" I used to get from district supervisors when I taught high school. I sometimes thought I was reading someone else's report since what I was reading was so at odds with how I was sure I was coming across.

We seldom visit one anothers' classrooms in college, or do so only to produce the perfunctory peer evaluation required for personnel actions. To get an honest opinion about your teaching from a colleague, the visit and the discussions following must be absolutely—one hundred percent—private and confidential. The slightest possibility that any suggested improvement might find its way into a personnel folder will put an end to what could be a highly significant and rewarding interaction. The relative ages of teacher and observer are not of much concern here. You never get too old to have a mentor. The nice thing about a videotape is that you and a colleague can watch it over beer and pretzels, stop it any time, or replay interesting or humorous parts.

A videotape is a particularly good way to test the effects of any change one might make in pedagogy or teaching style. If the camera operator has done a good job of including views of students, you can get a qualitative comparison of student involvement, say before and after a small-group, mid-period review or problem-solving session. Whether it's in my own class or a videotape of someone else's, the sight of a big group of students sitting or standing in small clusters and struggling, sometimes noisily, with some question or problem, convinces me that this is time very well spent. I invariably find that students are more willing, occasionally eager, to talk about content immediately after they and their study partners have spent some class time struggling with a question.

Having It All

Talks, articles, and books that intend to promote improved college teaching are sometimes received with the skepticism one normally associates with "other-world experiences." "Well and good," the young assistant professor or the busy researcher might say, "but I live in the real world." The real world continues with unrelenting ferocity to be one of "publish or perish" until at long last we find ourselves both publishing and perishing, to paraphrase Howard Nemerov from the poem, *A Full Professor*. The debates over student evaluations and whether they tell us anything true and useful about teaching pale beside those on the relative merits of teaching and research, or whether one individual should be or can be superlative in both, and even whether one has anything to do with the other. Page Smith (1990) is well known for his dyspeptic views on most university-based research. He more or less summed up his position when he wrote: "It can be said unequivocally that good teaching is far more complex, difficult, and demanding than mediocre research, which may explain why professors try so hard to avoid it." Many, obviously, will argue with that assertion, but they would have to agree, I suspect, that mediocre research is in fact more valued than excellent teaching.

College and university professors who excel at both teaching and research can be found and they are repeatedly held up as exemplars. In truth these are quite exceptional people—rarities even—and trying to emulate them presumes a great deal. As John Henry Newman said (quoted in Pelikan 1992), "To discover and to teach are distinct functions; they are also distinct gifts, and are not commonly found united in the same person."

Furthermore, the motivation to put time and effort into teaching and interacting with undergraduates must be found within the individual teacher; rarely will incentive come from colleagues or college administrators. The ethos that was long pervasive in research institutions has permeated even the smaller colleges, where published papers—particularly if they promise funding for further research—are highly valued. Excellent teaching, on the other hand, never gets its dollar value even estimated. Joseph

Lowman (1995) is clearly an earnest and tireless proponent of good teaching, but he also sees the problem, and I can do no better than quote his sad but realistic summation:

> Assistant professors at most schools must become minimally competent teachers in order to be promoted, but outstanding teaching will not offset a poor publication record. A better way to attain tenure would be to avoid being a poor teacher and do all you can to excel in the kinds of scholarship valued by your institution.

Sadly, a university is not the most congenial place for teachers.

Disturbing also is the possibility that putting effort into planning and thinking about teaching well is a luxury that only older tenured faculty can afford. It might turn out that any overall improvement in college teaching may have to come from that quarter.

Nevertheless, I would recommend to the younger professoriate a fine book by Donald Jarvis, *Junior Faculty Development: A Handbook* (1991). Jarvis notes, and quotes research sources to show, that research that is perfectly commendable in quantity and quality does not, in fact, demand as much time as is generally believed. A case can be made that the law of diminishing returns is alive and well in the matter of time spent on research. He suggests that spending more than about a third of one's active week on research does not result in commensurate productivity. Nor does "released time" increase the amount of research that gets done. The better researchers, he finds, concentrate their efforts in whatever blocks of time are available.

By the same token, I would suggest that teaching of high effectiveness does not require so very much more time than would the more indifferent variety. Few instructors need a lot of time to relearn what they are about to teach. Nor does it take much time to sketch out a plan of action for each class period, using the ideas suggested earlier. What does take time is reading student papers and exams, and the office hours that sometimes become tutorials. Where these activities end up on one's priorities list is, I suspect, some indication of the importance we place on student learning. I have for some time now believed that "not enough time" was something of a proxy for "not a high priority." When teaching is terribly important, the time it might take to do it well will always be found.

Second (Third and Fourth) Opinions

The pronoun *I* has appeared often in these pages, as have many personal observations and suggestions. In fact, there are no original ideas at all in this book. Even my unorthodox and clinical definitions of teaching, learning, and education were developed completely out of reflections on Jacques Barzun's marvelous book, *Begin Here* (1991). My fixation on language flows directly out of *Teaching as A Subversive Activity* by Neil Postman and Charles Weingartner (1969). A lot can be learned by reading.

But what is called the literature on matters educational is staggeringly massive and discouragingly diverse. I would divide this literature, somewhat crudely, into research and reflection; and divide the research, equally crudely, into small scale and large scale. Much of the research is impressive because it reports numerical confidence levels and differences in outcomes that are statistically significant. Educational research is said to be based on theory, but that theory, as I remarked earlier, is more akin to hypothesis. Much of educational research is the testing of hypotheses to see if they are deserving of the much devalued title, theory.

The amount of small-scale research that gets published is impressive. And it's the small-scale research I tend to distrust. These are frequently reports on the effects of a technique, or a method, or an experimental program, and generally involve a small number of people and a modest time frame. And they do seem, as one gimlet-eyed reviewer said, "doomed to succeed," particularly if the project is designed, carried out, and evaluated by the same person(s).

Then there is the large-scale research. The granddaddy of large-scale research is Alexander Astin's ongoing study of the effects of a variety of college experiences on learning. I trust large-scale research in most cases because it tends to ask simple questions about nodal problems and is not designed to sell anything. An important outcome of large-scale research is that, in many cases, it verifies something your grandmother would have said. Astin's study, for example, proved what everyone knew; you'll do better in college if you get to know your teachers, and if you and your friends study together instead of watching television. The impressive study on reading by Anne Cunningham and Keith Stanovich (1998) showed that the more you read the better reader you become, and better readers learn more.

Large-scale research frequently bears out the truth of convictions arrived at empirically by perceptive and insightful teachers—the reflective literature. The work of Cunningham and Stanovich, for example, demonstrates the wisdom of Postman's 1969 assertion that "learning is languaging."

So, for someone simply looking for something to stimulate their thinking about teaching I would recommend Neil Postman, Jacques Barzun, William James, Gilbert Highet, Rudolph Weingartner, and Joseph Lowman for straightforward writing, good reading, and advice you won't have to worry about. (See annotated bibliography for a brief description of some recommended readings.)

Also, surprisingly straightforward and hard hitting ideas come to any of us who are members of the American Federation of Teachers in the form of the quarterly journal, *American Educator* (*AE*). A couple times a year, at least, something relevant and useful for college teachers appears in the pages of *AE*. It appeals to me because of its courageous editorial staff. *AE* is often the first to say out loud, "the emperor has no clothes." So it was that Elizabeth McPike (1998), reviewing the reading problem, could write:

> The debate over whether reading is acquired 'naturally,' more or less like learning to speak, is over; reading requires explicit instruction. The debate over what role skilled decoding plays in reading comprehension is over; we know it is central.

So for the typical college professor not steeped in pedagogical theory, there is still much that can be learned by reading. But you need good instincts—you can't believe *everything* you read. For readers interested in more in-depth analyses of pedagogical literature I heartily recommend E. D. Hirsch, Jr. (1996) and Bonnie Grossen (1996). Their caveats and recommendations are more finely-reasoned and substantiated than those presented here.

Why Should I Bother?

Teaching well is hard work. It requires effort to learn students' names, patience to repeat over and again what they should already know, to urge them to study in groups and to coach them in the practice, to read their garbled syntax, and to listen to their complaints. Upperclassmen may appreciate us, but first-year students can be a thankless burden, at least at the beginning. Why should we bother?

Richard Dawkins (1976) wrote a most influential book called *The Selfish Gene*, in which he directed the world's attention to the linear passage and spread of genes across generations. Half our genes come from each parent and one-fourth from each grandparent, one-eighth from each great grandparent and so on. Half our genes will end up in our children, one-fourth in our grandchildren, one-eighth in our great grandchildren and so on. Interesting stuff to think about. But Dawkins realized that there has been, since the evolution of intelligence and speech, another kind of transmission down through generations. Ideas were going from head to head. He adapted the word *memes* as a kind of mental equivalent of genes. Memes are not a "brute reality," to use John Searle's expression, as a gene is, but the word itself represents a real phenomenon. We learn with the help of our teachers, who learned with the help of theirs.

But memes, like genes, can drift through a population randomly, or become settled in small pockets here and there. Elmore (1996) lamented the fact that good teaching ideas do not spread through the educational community replacing lesser ones, the way an advantageous gene normally would. The educational community is not truly competitive and so does not select for the best pedagogy. Similarly, good teaching may well be wasted on some, but it will do its work on others and good things will be passed on to some, at least, of the next generation. As Highet (1966) said upon reflecting on the almost mysterious quality that infused good teachers, "It gave them that power over their pupils which extended to all kinds of young men and women, from different countries and classes, and which continued to work long after [their teachers] were dead."

Teachers who make a difference are not, unfortunately, sparks dropping into dry grass. They are more like the occasional mountain laurel that manages to thrive in the midst of things bigger and lesser and lifts the spirit when chanced upon.

In this era of distance learning, accountability, productivity, cost effectiveness, and Total Quality Management, any realistic teacher might ask whether it's in anybody's best interest to work hard at inspiring students, prodding them, and languaging them. Maybe hypertext *is* the answer? I'll give the penultimate word on that matter to Clifford Stoll (1995) who asks us to "think of your own experience: name three multimedia programs that actually inspired you. Now name three teachers that made a difference in your life."

As the kids say, Bingo!

Assignment 1

School Name
Course Name/number
Date issued
Assignment # (   )

Imagine that your older sister (a highly intelligent History major) has donated blood, and has found out what her blood type is. She asks you one day, "Just what is it that makes one blood type different from another? What makes type A different, for example, from type O?" She also wonders how something like blood type can be inherited.

Your job is to come up with an essay of two or three pages that answers her questions. Keep the following facts well in mind:

1. Big words do not explain anything, particularly to someone who does not know much biology. Words like *allele* and *epitope* will not help at all.

2. The reader is fairly smart and will not be confused by words like "protein" or "enzyme."

3. The question in no way concerns transfusions.

4. Keep well in mind *exactly* what it is we inherit from our parents.

Remember that this is not a generic essay on blood, but an attempt to answer two very specific questions. It would be very helpful to discuss this assignment with the people you normally study with and to compare ideas. You should also e-mail me specific questions if you get stuck. But remember, the actual writing must be done by each individual. A group-written assignment will not be acceptable.

The first draft, which will not be graded, is due one week from today. Both the first and final drafts must be typed or machine printed. Hand-written papers will be returned without comment.

Assignment 2

School Name
Course Name/number
Date issued
Assignment # (   )

Imagine that you and your study group were exploring an uninhabited island when your cruise ship went off and left you there for a week (assume lots of bananas, coconuts, etc.) At the end of the second day you've run out of conversation and are sitting on the beach looking at the moon. Someone recalls that the moon moves around the earth once every 28/29 days, and the earth rotates on its axis once every 24 days. An argument breaks out as to whether the moon orbits the earth in the same direction as the earth rotates, or in the opposite direction.

Using only what you might find on an uninhabited island and what you would likely have brought with you (and that would not include a computer, a telescope, or an encyclopedia) design an experiment that would conclusively demonstrate which is correct, that the moon orbits the earth in the same or the opposite direction as the earth rotates. Write a description of your experiment, your audience being those who had a wrong opinion on the matter. It must persuade them of their error.

As always, confer and agree on the method, but write your own description of the process. Include convincing arguments as to why this procedure would give an answer. Perhaps a diagram would be helpful. If the weather is cooperative you might even want to actually try your idea.

First draft, typed or machine printed, is due one week from today. The second draft will be graded.

Listed here are only those items referred to in the text. It is not a complete listing of the many articles and books that were consulted or that influenced my thinking during the writing. Immediately following is a short annotated bibliography of works that are particularly recommended.

Ambady, N. and R. Rosenthal. 1993. "Half a Minute: Predicting Teacher Evaluations From Thin Slices of Nonverbal Behavior and Physical Attractivness." *Journal of Personality and Social Psychology* 64: 431–41.

Anderson, Martin. 1992. *Imposters in the Temple: American Intellectuals Are Destroying Our Universities and Cheating Our Students of Their Future.* (New York: Simon and Schuster).

Armstrong, William H. 1997. "Learning to Listen." *American Educator* (winter 1997–98): 24–47. (Exerpt from *Study Is Hard Work.* D. R. Godine, 1995.)

Arons, Arnold. 1990. *A Guide to Introductory Physics Teaching.* (New York: Wiley and Sons).

Astin, Alexander W. 1993. *What Matters in College?* (San Francisco: Jossey-Bass).

Barr, Robert N. and John Tagg. 1995. "From Teaching to Learning: A New Paradigm for Undergraduate Education." *Change* (November/December): 12–25.

Barzun, Jacques. 1991. *Begin Here: The Forgotten Conditions of Teaching and Learning.* (Chicago: University of Chicago Press).

Baumeister, Roy F. 1996. "Should Schools Try to Boost Self-Esteem?" *American Educator* (summer 1996): 14–43.

Bloom, Allan. 1993. *Love and Friendship.* (New York: Simon and Schuster).

Bok, Derek. 1986. *Higher Learning.* (Cambridge: Harvard University Press).

Brookfield, Stephen D. 1990. *The Skillful Teacher: On Technique, Trust, and Responsiveness in the Classroom.* (San Francisco: Jossey-Bass).

Bruner, Jerome S. 1968. *Toward a Theory of Instruction.* (New York: W. W. Norton).

Changeux, Jean-Pierre. 1985. *Neuronal Man: The Biology of Mind.* Translated by Laurence Garey. (New York: Oxford University Press).

Cromer, Alan. 1997. *Connected Knowledge.* (New York: Oxford University Press).

Cuban, Larry. 1984. *How Teachers Taught: Constancy and Change in American Classrooms 1890–1980.* (New York: Longman, 1984).

Cunningham, Anne E. and Keith E. Stanovich. 1998. "What Reading Does for the Mind." *American Educator* (spring/summer): 8–15.

Dawkins, Richard. 1976. *The Selfish Gene.* (New York: Oxford University Press).

Dewey, John. 1963. *Experience and Education.* (New York: Collier.)

Dunn, Rita Stafford and Kenneth Dunn. 1978. *Teaching Students Through Their Individual Learning Styles: A Practical Approach.* (Reston, VA: Reston Publishing).

Dunn, Rita and Shirley A. Griggs. 1988. *Learning Styles: Quiet Revolution in American Secondary Schools.* (Reston, VA: National Association of Secondary School Principals).

Eble, Kenneth E. 1972. *Professors As Teachers.* (San Francisco: Jossey-Bass).

———. 1983. *The Aims of College Teaching.* (San Francisco: Jossey-Bass.

———. 1988. *The Craft of Teaching.* (San Francisco: Jossey-Bass).

Edelman, Gerald M. 1989. *The Remembered Present: A Biological Theory of Consciousness.* New York: Basic Book.

Ehrmann, Stephen C. 1995. "Asking the Right Questions: What Does Research Tell Us About Technology and Higher Learning?" *Change* (March/April): 20–27.

Elmore, Richard F. 1996. "Getting to Scale with Good Educational Practice." *Harvard Educational Review* 66, 1 (spring): 1–26.

Erickson, Bette L. and Diane W. Strommer. 1991. *Teaching College Freshmen.* (San Francisco: Jossey-Bass).

Flanagan, Owen. 1991. *The Science of The Mind.* (Cambridge: MIT Press.)

Fulwiler, Toby. 1987. *Teaching with Writing.* (Portsmouth, N.H.: Boynton/Cook).

Geohegan, William. 1995. "Stuck at the Barricades: Can Information Technology Really Enter the Mainstream of Teaching and Learning?" *Change* (March/April): 30–31.

Grossen, Bonnie. 1996. "Making Research Serve the Profession." *American Educator* (fall): 4–27.

Healy, Jane M. 1990. *Endangered Minds: Why Our Children Don't Think.* (New York: Simon and Schuster).

Highet, Gilbert. 1966. *The Art of Teaching.* (New York: Alfred A. Knopf).

Hirsch Jr. , E. D. 1996a. *The Schools We Need: And Why We Don't Have Them.* (New York: Doubleday).

———. 1996b. "Reality's Revenge: Research and Ideology." *American Educator* (fall): 4–46.

James, William. 1904. *Talks to Teachers.* (New York: Henry Holt.)

Jarvis, Donald K. 1991. *Junior Faculty Development: A Handbook.* (New York: Modern Language Association of America).

Katz, Joseph and Mildred Henry. 1988. *Turning Professors Into Teachers.* (New York: Macmillan).

Klivington, Kenneth. 1989. *The Science of Mind*. (Cambridge: The M.I.T. Press).

Kozulin, Alex. 1990. *Vygotsky's Psychology*. (Cambridge: Harvard University Press).

Leamnson, Robert N. 1995. *Learning Your Way Through College*. (San Francisco: Wadsworth).

Lerner, Barbara. 1996. "Self-Esteem and Excellence: The Choice and the Paradox." *American Educator* (summer): 9–41.

Light, Richard. 1990. *The Harvard Assessment Seminars: Explorations with Students and Faculty about Teaching, Learning, and Student Life*. (First Report) (Cambridge, MA: Graduate School of Education).

———. 1992. *The Harvard Assessment Seminars: Explorations with Students and Faculty about Teaching, Learning, and Student Life*. (Second Report) (Cambridge: Graduate School of Education).

Lowman, Joseph. 1995. *Mastering The Techniques of Teaching*. (San Francisco: Jossey-Bass).

Matsuzawa, Tetsuro. 1996. "Chimpanzee Intelligence in Nature and in Captivity: Isomorphism of Symbol use and Tool Use" in *Great Ape Studies*. W. C. McGrew, W. C. Marchant, L. F. Toshisada, and Nishida Toshisada, eds. (Cambridge: Cambridge University Press).

McCullough, David. 1995. "A Sense of Proportion" *American Educator* (spring): 38–45.

McPike, Elizabeth. 1998. "The Unique Power of Reading and How to Unleash It." *American Educator* (spring/summer): 4–5.

Meyers, Chet, and Thomas B. Jones. 1993. *Promoting Active Learning: Strategies for the College Classroom*. (San Francisco: Jossey-Bass).

Naftulin, C. H. , J. E. Ware and F. A. Connelly. 1973. "The Doctor Fox Lecture: A Paradigm of Educational Seduction," *Journal of Medical Education* 48: 630–35.

Nickerson, Raymond S, David N. Perkins and Edward E. Smith. 1985. *The Teaching of Thinking*. (Hillsdale, NJ: Lawrence Erlbaum).

Ong, Walter J. 1982. *Orality and Literacy: The Technologizing of the Word*. (New York: Methuen).

Oppenheimer, Todd. 1997. "The Computer Delusion." *The Atlantic Monthly* (July): 45–62.

Ortega y Gasset, José. 1987. *Psychological Investigations*. (New York: Norton).

Pelikan, Jaroslav. 1992. *The Idea of the University: A Re-examination*. (New Haven: Yale University Press).

Pinker, Steven. 1997. *How the Mind Works*. New York: W. W. Norton.

Plotkin, Henry. 1994. *Darwin Machines and the Nature of Knowledge*. (Cambridge: Harvard University Press).

Postman, Neil and Charles Weingartner. 1969. *Teaching as a Subversive Activity*. (New York: Delacorte Press).

Postman, Neil. 1992. *Technopoly: The Surrender of Culture to Technology*. (New York: Knopf).

———. 1995. *The End of Education*. (New York: Knopf).

Restak, Richard M. 1994. *The Modular Brain*. (New York: Simon and Schuster.)

Rodin, Miriam and Burton Rodin. 1972. "Student Evaluations of Teachers: Students Rate Most Highly Instructors from Whom They Learn Least." *Science* 177: 1164–66.

Rowe, Mary-Budd. 1987. "Wait Time: Slowing Down May Be a Way of Speeding Up." *American Educator* (spring): 38–43.

Russell, David R. 1991. *Writing in the Academic Disciplines, 1870–1990*. (Southern Illinois University Press).

Schell, Jonathan. 1996. "The Uncertain Leviathan." *The Atlantic Monthly* (August): 70–78.

Schroeder, Charles C. 1993. "New Students—New Learning Styles." *Change* (September/October): 21–26.

Schwab, J. J. 1978. "Eros and Education" in *Science, Curriculum, and Liberal Education: Selected Essays*. (Chicago: University of Chicago Press).

Searle, John R. 1992. *The Rediscovery of the Mind*. (Cambridge: The MIT Press).

Singal, Daniel. 1991. "The Other Crisis in American Education." *The Atlantic Monthly* (November): 59–74.

Smith, Page. 1984. *Dissenting Opinions*. (San Francisco: North Point Press).

———. 1990. *Killing the Spirit: Higher Education in America*. (New York: Viking Press).

Smyth, W. J. 1986. *A Rationale for Teachers' Critical Pedagogy: A Handbook*. (Victoria, Australia: Deakin University Press).

Sternberg, Robert J. 1997. *Thinking Styles*. (Cambridge: Cambridge University Press).

Stevens, Charles F. 1993. "Quantal Release of Neurotransmitter and Long-Term Potentiation." *Cell Neuron: Review Supplement to Cell 72/Neuron 10* (January): 55–63.

Stigler, James W. and Harold W. Stevenson. 1991. "How Asian Teachers Polish Each Lesson to Perfection." *American Educator* (1991): 12–47.

Stoll, Clifford. 1995. *Silicon Snake Oil: Second Thoughts on the Information Highway*. (New York: Doubleday).

Stunkel, Kenneth R. 1998. "The Lecture: A Powerful Tool for Intellectual Liberation." *The Chronicle of Higher Education* (June 26).

Tiberius, Richard G. , and Janet M Billson. 1991. "The Social Context of Teaching and Learning" in *New Directions for Teaching and Learning* R. Menges and M. Svinicki (eds.). (San Francisco: Jossey-Bass).

Trout, Paul A. 1997. "What The Numbers Mean." *Change* (September/October): 25–30.

Walvoord, Barbara E. and L. P. McCarthy. 1990. In *Thinking and Writing in College: A Naturalistic Study of Students in Four Disciplines.* Barbara E. Fassler Walvoord *et al.* (Urbana IL: National Council of Teachers of English).

Weingartner, Rudolph H. 1992. *Undergraduate Education: Goals and Means.* (New York: Macmillan).

Welsh, Patrick. 1992. "It Takes Two to Tango." *American Educator* (spring): 18–46.

Williams, Wendy M. and Stephen J. Ceci. 1997. "How'm I Doing? Problems With Student Ratings of Instructors and Courses." *Change* (September/ October): 13–23.

Wilson, Kenneth G. , and Bennett Daviss. 1994. *Redesigning Education.* (New York: Henry Holt).

Zinsser, William. 1988. *Writing to Learn.* (New York: Harper and Row.)

ANNOTATED BIBLIOGRAPHY

Here is a list in no particular order of books I feel comfortable in recommending, each with a brief annotation. When looking over the list I realized that there were certain properties these books had in common, those I suspect that made them appealing to me. All the authors are remarkably insightful, and none is afraid to let you know where they stand on any issue. You will find very little "but on the other hand" fence straddling in these books. None of them is a compendium of theories and practices (although Lowman does cover a lot of ground). They are written well, therefore they read well, particularly for those unaccustomed to literature in the field of pedagogy. Seldom will you find yourself jumping ahead because a paragraph is beginning to churn.

TALKS TO TEACHERS (ON PSYCHOLOGY) *by William James (1904).*

The language may be nineteenth century but the ideas and insights in this collection of essays are absolutely timeless. James always went to the heart of the matter. Few people since have seen so clearly what it means to learn, or what a teacher must do to inspire it. He anticipated everything.

THE ART OF TEACHING *by Gilbert Highet (1966).*

Where James is precise and analytical, Highet is large-hearted and loving. The edition I use is a 1966 printing but the original came out in 1950. I read this book in two afternoons (later spending two more days making notes) and at the end wished that I could have been one of Highet's students. There is nothing to equal Highet for an appreciation of the almost frighteningly personal nature of teaching.

UNDERGRADUATE EDUCATION: GOALS AND MEANS
by Rudolph Weingartner (1992).

Read Weingartner for a thorough exposition of the multiple facets of undergraduate education. The writing is as elegant as one is likely to find—complex but clear. There is little that is prescriptive here—the scope is broad ranging and philosophical. This is a book to linger over, to savor, and to think about when sorting out one's personal philosophy of teaching.

BEGIN HERE: THE FORGOTTEN CONDITIONS OF TEACHING AND LEARNING *by Jacques Barzun (1991).*

The grand old man, the *bête noire* of progressive "educationists," is at his best here. This small book is a collection of essays going back many years, but each updated with a 1991 introduction. A fond disciple of James, Barzun saw his job as casting a thousand stones at the meddlers. This is "give no quarter" writing sure to offend nearly everyone one place or another. But once he has our attention, the open minded reader will realize that here is a man who understands learning and knows what it takes to teach well. Obviously not prescriptive—just inspirational. The writing, it needn't be said, is masterful.

MASTERING THE TECHNIQUES OF TEACHING *by Joseph Lowman (1995).*

Don't be misled by the title. While there is indeed practical advice here, the unmistakable underpinning throughout is the emotional, personal, and dramatic nature of the classroom. I was both surprised and taken by the impression it made on me. If you read it in a receptive spirit you are not likely afterward to be able to see the classroom as a place to recite one's discipline. For all its calm style and unpretentious title, it does get the juices going.

TEACHING AS A SUBVERSIVE ACTIVITY *by Neil Postman and Charles Weingartner (1969).*

Neil Postman is so bright and so perceptive, anything he writes is easily recommended (try also *Amusing Ourselves to Death* and *Technopoly*). If I have not convinced you of the connection of learning to language, read Postman and Weingartner. Postman here (and elsewhere) addresses what might be a nodal problem in some aspects of progressive education, i.e. letting the preoccupation with student-centered teaching drift into an accommodation of students as we find them when we should be trying to change them. Solid ideas in a light engaging style.

WHAT MATTERS IN COLLEGE *by Alexander Astin (1993).*

THE HARVARD ASSESSMENT SEMINARS *by Richard Light (1990–92).*

These items are recommended together and only for those interested in the research and statistics that back up two solid bits of advice to students: get connected with your teachers and talk academics with your peers. Not exactly page-turners, but good for solid research data.

ENDANGERED MINDS: WHY OUR CHILDREN DON'T THINK
by Jane M. Healy (1990).

THE SCHOOLS WE NEED: AND WHY WE DON'T HAVE THEM
by J. D. Hirsch, Jr. (1996).

Again, these are recommended as a pair because they both address a problem indirectly related to college teaching: how our students got to be the way they are. Hirsch's book is informational and will help understand chapter 4 of the present book. Healy's book is very highly recommended, even thought it concerns quite young students, because it shows over and again how the deprivation of language experience can undermine subsequent attempts to educate.

THE SKILLFUL TEACHER *by Stephen D. Brookfield (1990).*

Not quite so vibrant and forceful as some of the previous, but refreshingly honest and straightforward. The style is chatty and sometimes rambling and it makes the list primarily because of chapter 14, "Some Truths About Skillful Teaching." This chapter consists of a series of mini-essays on some seventeen relevant aspects of good teaching. Read chapter 14 if nothing else.

INDEX